SHEPHERD'S NOTES

Shepherd's Notes Titles Available

SHEPHERD'S NOTES COMMENTARY SERIES

Old Testament

New Testament

SHEPHERD'S NOTES CHRISTIAN CLASSICS

SHEPHERD'S NOTES — BIBLE SUMMARY SERIES

SHEPHERD'S NOTES

When you need a guide through the Scriptures

Hebrews

HOLMAN
REFERENCE

NASHVILLE, TENNESSEE

Shepherds Notes—*Hebrews*
© 1998 B&H Publishing Group, Nashville, Tennessee
All rights reserved
Printed in the United States of America

ISBN# 978-0-8054-9336-8

Dewey Decimal Classification: 227.870
Subject Heading: BIBLE. N.T. HEBREWS
Library of Congress Card Catalog Number: 98-27120

Library of Congress Cataloging-in-Publication Data

Gould, Dana, 1951–
    Hebrews / Dana Gould, editor [i.e. author]
       p. cm. — (Shepherd's notes)
    Includes bibliographical references
    ISBN 0-8054-9336-0 (pbk.)
    1. Bible N.T. Hebrews—Study and teaching.   I. Title
II. Series
BS2775.5.G68 1998
227'.8707—dc21

                                           98-27120
                                            CIP

15 16 17 18 19   20 19 18 17 16

CONTENTS

Dear Reader:

Shepherd's Notes are designed to give you a quick, step-by-step overview of every book of the Bible. They are not meant to be substitutes for the biblical text; rather, they are study guides intended to help you explore the wisdom of Scripture in personal or group study and to apply that wisdom successfully in your own life.

Shepherd's Notes guide you through the main themes of each book of the Bible and illuminate fascinating details through appropriate commentary and reference notes. Historical and cultural background information brings the Bible into sharper focus.

Six different icons, used throughout the series, call your attention to historical-cultural information, Old Testament and New Testament references, word pictures, unit summaries, and personal application for everyday life.

Whether you are a novice or a veteran at Bible study, I believe you will find *Shepherd's Notes* a resource that will take you to a new level in your mining and applying the riches of Scripture.

In Him,

David R. Shepherd
Editor-in-Chief

DESIGNED FOR THE BUSY USER

Shepherd's Notes for Hebrews is designed to provide an easy-to-use tool for getting a quick handle on a Bible book's important features and for gaining an understanding of the message of Hebrews. Information available in more difficult-to-use reference works has been incorporated into the *Shepherd's Notes* format. This brings you the benefits of many more advanced and expensive works packed into one small volume.

Shepherd's Notes are for laymen, pastors, teachers, small-group leaders and participants, as well as the classroom student. Enrich your personal study or quiet time. Shorten your class or small-group preparation time as you gain valuable insights in the truths of God's Word that you can pass along to your students or group members.

DESIGNED FOR QUICK ACCESS

Those with time restraints will especially appreciate the timesaving features built in the *Shepherd's Notes*. All features are intended to aid a quick and concise encounter with the crux of the message.

Concise Commentary. Hebrews is unique among the New Testament writings and deserves to be read and studied over a lifetime. *Shepherd's Notes* provides you with an overview of this letter and will enable you to find sections and passages where you would like to spend more time. Short sections provide quick "snapshots" of passages, highlighting important points and other information.

Outlined Text. A comprehensive outline covers the entire text of Hebrews. This is a valuable feature for following the narrative's flow and allows for a quick, easy way to locate a particular passage.

Shepherd's Notes. These summary statements appear at the close of every key section of the narrative. While functioning in part as a quick summary, they also deliver the essence of the message presented in the sections they cover.

Icons. Various icons in the margin highlight recurring themes in Hebrews and aid in selective searching or tracing of those themes.

Sidebars and Charts. These specially selected features provide additional background information to your study or preparation. These include definitions as well as cultural, historical, and biblical insights.

Maps. These are placed at appropriate places in the book to aid your understanding and study of a text or passage.

Questions to Guide Your Study. These thought-provoking questions and discussion starters are designed to encourage interaction with the truth and principles of God's Word.

In addition to the above features, study aids have been included at the back of the book for those readers who desire more information and resources for working through Hebrews. These include chapter outlines for studying Hebrews and a list of reference sources used for this volume, which includes many works that allow the reader to extend the scope of his or her study of this letter.

DESIGNED TO WORK FOR YOU

Personal Study. Using the *Shepherd's Notes* with a passage of Scripture can enlighten your study and take it to a new level. At your fingertips is information that would require searching several volumes to find. In addition, many points of application occur throughout the volume, contributing to personal growth.

Teaching. Outlines frame the text of Hebrews and provide a logical presentation of the message. Shepherd's Notes icons provide summary statements for presenting the essence of key points and events. Personal Application icons point out personal application of the message of Hebrews, and Historical Context icons indicate where background information is supplied.

Group Study. Shepherd's Notes can be an excellent companion volume to use for gaining a quick but accurate understanding of the message of a Bible book. Each group member can benefit by having his or her own copy. The *Shepherd's Note's* format accommodates the study of or the tracing of the themes throughout Hebrews. Leaders may use its flexible features to prepare for group sessions or to use during group sessions. Questions to Guide Your Study can spark discussion of the key points and truths of Hebrews.

LIST OF MARGIN ICONS USED IN HEBREWS

Shepherd's Notes. Placed at the end of each section, a capsule statement provides the reader with the essence of the message of that section.

Historical Context. To indicate background information—historical, biographical, cultural—and provide insight on the understanding or interpretation of a passage.

Old Testament Reference. To indicate an Old Testament passage that illuminates a passage in Hebrews.

New Testament Reference. Used when the writer refers to New Testament passages that are either fulfilled prophecy, an antitype of an Old Testament type, or a New Testament text which in some other way illuminates the passages under discussion.

Personal Application. Used when the text provides a personal or universal application of truth.

Word Picture. Indicates that the meaning of a specific word or phrase is illustrated so as to shed light on it.

INTRODUCTION

The book of Hebrews is anonymous in that the author's name is not mentioned. Despite the difficulties in determining the author, the book's majestic picture of Christ commended its contents to the early church.

The writer of Hebrews presented Christ as superior to the Old Testament prophets, angels, Moses, Joshua, and Aaron. He laced magnificent discussions of Christ's person and work into frightening passages that warn against apostasy (1:1–2:4). The superiority of Christ led the writer to appeal for faith (chap. 2), stamina (12:3–11), and good works (13:16).

HEBREWS IN A NUTSHELL

PURPOSE	TO URGE CHRISTIANS TO CONTINUE THEIR PROFESSION OF CHRIST.
Key Words	"Better, Superior." Christ is superior to the angels, Moses, and Aaron. Hebrews has a *better* priesthood, covenant, and sacrifice.
Theme	Jesus Christ is the High Priest who offered Himself as the perfect sacrifice for sins.
Major Doctrines	The person of Christ—both His humanity and His deity; Christ's atonement for our sins.

AUTHOR

Hebrews is anonymous, and attempts to establish its authorship are conjecture. Nowhere in its thirteen chapters does Hebrews mention its options. The letter's readers obviously knew who the writer was, but the name has not been preserved for us.

The early church was uncertain about the author of this anonymous letter. Eastern Christendom usually regarded Paul as the author, while Western Christendom doubted Pauline authorship and initially excluded Hebrews from the canon because of this uncertainty.

The early church historian Eusebius quoted the biblical scholar Origen as saying, "Who it was that really wrote the epistle Hebrews, God only knows" (*Eccelesiastical History,* 6.25). Despite this verdict, many varied opinions about the authorship have arisen.

Christians in the Eastern Roman Empire regarded Paul as the author. Hebrews contains statements similar to Paul's view of the preexistence and creatorship of Christ (cp. Heb. 1:1–4 with Col. 1:15–17). Both Hebrews 8:6 and 2 Corinthians 3:4–11 discuss the New Covenant. These factors inclined some observers to consider Paul as the author.

Christians in the Western Roman Empire originally questioned Pauline authorship of Hebrews. They observed that the statement of 2:3 suggests that the author was not an apostle. Also the Old Testament quotations in Hebrews come from the Greek Septuagint, but Paul used both the Hebrew text and the Septuagint. Furthermore, none of Paul's other writings are anonymous, and the polished Greek style of Hebrews does not resemble the explosive, dynamic style of most of Paul's writings. Shortly before A.D. 400, Christian leaders in the West extended acceptance to the book of Hebrews. They absorbed it into the Pauline collection of writings without distinguishing it from the rest.

Tertullian advocated Barnabas as the author of Hebrews. Barnabas's background as a Levite would have qualified him to write the book, but support for his authorship is lacking in the early church. Martin Luther suggested Apollos as the author. In Apollos's favor is his reputation for eloquence (Acts 18:24), but against him is the absence of early church tradition accepting him as author. Some have suggested Luke as the author. His knowledge of Greek would favor him, but Luke was a Gentile. The outlook of Hebrews is definitely Jewish. The nineteenth-century church historian Adolph Harnack mentioned Priscilla, the wife of Aquila, as the author. She and her husband would have known Pauline theology and Jewish practice, but the early church was silent about nominating her as author.

Modern Greek texts of Hebrews bear the title "To the Hebrews." It is best to accept this title and recognize that we cannot know for sure who wrote Hebrews. Despite our ignorance of the author, we can use and understand what he wrote.

AUDIENCE

The title "to the Hebrews" reflects the conviction that Jewish Christians were the original readers of the writing. Frequent appeals to the Old Testament, an extensive knowledge of Jewish ritual, and the warning not to return to Jewish ritual support this conviction.

One might feel that the Jewish Christians who read Hebrews lived in Palestine. According to 2:3, however, the readers may not have seen nor heard Jesus during His earthly ministry. The verse suggests that the readers had been dependent on the first hearers of the Christian message to share it with them. Doubtless, most Palestinian Christians had heard Jesus preach and teach.

According to 6:10, the readers of Hebrews had resources enough to assist other believers; Palestinian Christians were poor and needed aid (Acts 11:27–30; Rom. 15:26). These facts indicate that the readers were not from Palestine.

The statement in 13:24, "Those from Italy send you their greetings," sounds as if Italians away from their home were returning greetings to friends in Rome. If this is true, Rome is the probable destination of the writing. A second fact favoring this view is that a knowledge of Hebrews first appears in Clement's First Epistle, which was written in Rome.

PURPOSE FOR WRITING

The purpose of Hebrews is closely linked to the identity of its recipients. All agree that the letter is written for Christians who are being urged to continue their profession of faith in Christ.

Wherever the recipients lived, they were well known to the writer. He described them as generous (6:10) but immature (5:11–14). He is aware of their persecution (10:32–34; 12:4), and he plans to visit them soon (13:19, 23).

The writer rebuked the readers for not meeting together often enough (10:24–25). They are in danger of lapsing into sin (3:12–14). Perhaps the readers were a Jewish-Christian group who had broken away from the chief body of Christians in the area. They were considering returning to Judaism to avoid persecution. The author wrote to warn them against such apostasy (6:4–9; 10:26–31) and to help them return to the mainstream of Christian fellowship.

DATE OF WRITING

The date of the writing of Hebrews is difficult to determine. We must date the book before A.D.

95, when Clement referred to it. The writer used present-tense verbs in 10:11 ("performs" and "offers") to describe the ministry of the priests in the Jerusalem Temple. This indicates that sacrifices were still being offered in the days of the writer.

The Roman army destroyed the Temple in A.D. 70. Persecution intensified as that day drew near (see 10:32–34). Timothy was still alive (13:23). The best option for the date is the mid-to-late 60s before the Romans destroyed the Temple.

LITERARY FORM

Opening. Letters in the New Testament period began with specific salutations and concluded with benedictions and farewells. They were written to meet needs in the life of the church. Hebrews has some, but not all, of these characteristics. The letter begins without a salutation and omits the naming of the author and addressees.

Language. The language of Hebrews is elegant and carefully constructed. Its excellent Greek (the language in which the letter was originally written) does not clearly show up in English translations that strive for readability.

Oratorical Style. Was the writer penning a letter to a specific group of Christians, or was the letter a summary of a sermon made available to several Christian congregations? "I do not have time to tell" (11:32) seems to indicate a sermon; however, the writer knew specific details about the congregation (5:11–12; 6:9–10; 10:32–34; 12:4; 13:7). This suggests a letter written to a specific location. The statement in 13:22 also requires that we view the writing as a letter penned in the style of an earnest warning to a specific congregation.

Closing. The book concludes with a benediction, some personal observations, and a farewell (13:20–25).

SPECIAL FEATURES OF LETTER TO THE HEBREWS

Its Original Greek Text. The Greek text of the letter to the Hebrews has high literary qualities and reflects an elegant vocabulary.

Its Use of Old Testament Quotations. It also makes frequent allusions to and quotes from the Old Testament. Some passages such as Psalm 110:1, 4 appear repeatedly (1:13; 6:20; 7:17, 21; 10:12–13). The quotations do not serve as mere confirmations of the author's opinions; they provide the foundation for the presentation itself.

Its Doctrines of Christ. The Christology of Hebrews is incredibly rich and varied. Over twenty titles or names are used for Christ. Both the humanity and the deity of Christ are emphasized in Hebrews.

Its Warnings. A group of five warnings appear in the argument of Hebrews. These warnings are found in 2:1–4; 3:7–4:13; 5:11–6:20; 10:26–39; and 12:15–29. The writer was anxious that his listeners pay special attention to the voice of the living God. Most of the warnings deal with the danger of neglecting the salvation in Christ or missing out on it because of unbelief, apostasy, or compromise.

THE DOCTRINES OF HEBREWS

The Letter to the Hebrews emphasizes the person of Christ. It presents a Jesus who is truly human (2:18), realistically tempted (4:15), and obedient to death (3:2; 13:12). The suffering of Jesus taught Him the value of obedience (5:8).

Hebrews also emphasizes the finality of Christ's work. The sacrifices offered by Jewish priests in the Temple reminded the worshipers of sin, but the sacrifice of Christ removed sin (10:1–4). The priests of Judaism repeatedly offered sacrifices that did not take away sin (10:11). Christ's single offering of Himself forever removed the sin that hindered fellowship with God (10:12–14).

THE THEOLOGICAL SIGNIFICANCE OF HEBREWS

The author of Hebrews pointed his readers to the superiority of Jesus Christ. He is superior to the prophets (1:1–3), superior to the angels (1:4–2:18), and to Moses (3:1–13). He provides a superior priesthood on the basis of a superior covenant (4:14–10:31). Not only is Jesus superior to the foundational aspects of Judaism, but He also is superior to any aspect of contemporary religion. This means that Jesus is not just one good option among many ways of drawing near to God; He is the *only* way. Because of the superiority of Jesus we must not neglect such a great salvation that He has provided with His sacrificial death (2:3; 10:1–18).

Jesus, the superior Savior, is also the superior Priest. We can come to Him in times of trouble, suffering, and struggle. In Him we will find a sympathetic Priest (4:14–16) who offers grace in time of need. Thus we can and should draw near to Him in worship (10:19–25), live by faith (11:1–40), persevere to the end (12:1–29), and live a life of love (13:1–25).

THE RELEVANCE OF HEBREWS FOR CHRISTIANS TODAY

Hebrews is among the least read, least studied, and least preached from books of the New Testament. Modern readers sometimes have problems with its descriptions of ancient religious practices. Readers in every century have been confused and disturbed by its harsh warnings. However, those who dig into Hebrews discover that it has much to say to us today.

Above all, Hebrews challenges us to be faithful to Christ, no matter what the cost. Fair-weather Christianity finds no comfort in the book of Hebrews. Our lukewarm complacency is shattered by its words of warning, and our faith is stirred by its words of challenge. We are warned against becoming too comfortable with this world and its values. We are reminded that we are pilgrims on the way to glory and that we are to live in light of the values of that eternal kingdom.

As we walk this pilgrim way, Christ is fully adequate to meet our needs. Through Him, we have access to God in prayer and worship, and we have a fellowship of mutual encouragement with others who are marching to Zion. Christ has passed this way Himself; therefore, He helps and encourages us as we encounter various trials and temptations.

BASIC OUTLINE FOR HEBREWS

  I. The Superiority of Christ over the Old Testament Prophets (1:1–2)

  II. The Superiority of Christ over Angels (1:4–2:18)

  III. The Superiority of Christ over Moses (3:1–19)

IV. The Superiority of Christ over Joshua
   (4:1–13)
 V. The Superiority of Christ over Aaron
   (4:14–10:18)
VI. The Practice of Spiritual Endurance
   (10:19–12:29)
VII. Final Exhortations (13:1–25)

QUESTIONS TO GUIDE YOUR STUDY

1. Who were the readers of the book of Hebrews?
2. What was the writer's purpose for his letter?
3. What key doctrines does the author address in this letter?
4. What is unique about Hebrews?
5. What in this letter makes it relevant to today's readers?

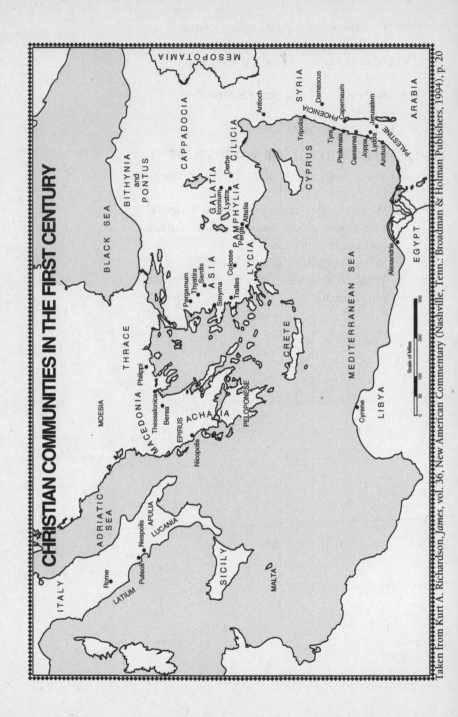

CHRISTIAN COMMUNITIES IN THE FIRST CENTURY

The revelation of God given through Christ is both superior and final. The writer's majestic descriptions of Jesus in these verses implies that in both *quality* and *quantity* God has no further revelation to give other than what He has already given in Jesus.

JESUS IS SUPERIOR TO THE PROPHETS (1:1–4)

God Spoke Through the Prophets (v. 1)

Without any salutation, the writer of Hebrews launched his letter. From the very first sentence, he issued a powerful proclamation of the good news of God through Jesus Christ the Son. This introduction is concise. At the same time, it is astoundingly broad in its scope. "God spoke to our forefathers through the prophets" (v. 1), leaves the clear impression the original readers of this letter were Jewish. The Hebrew prophets were God's spokesmen who uniquely brought the word of the Lord's judgment and the word of the Lord's loving-kindness to His chosen people.

The Hebrew people built their theology on the conviction that God *exists*, that He is *one*, and that *He has spoken*. The prophetic tradition was forward-looking. In that tradition, men like Amos and Micah and women like Miriam (Exod. 15:20) and Anna (Luke 2:36) were caught up by God's Spirit and compelled to proclaim His Word in a language clearly understood by the common people. As Amos said, "The lion has roared—who will not fear? The Sovereign Lord has spoken—who can but prophesy?" (Amos 3:8).

The prophets' saying, "This is what the Sovereign Lord says," was the standard that marked Israel's dynamic progression toward the Messiah. The prophets were both seers of the messianic hope and speakers for God concerning the coming revelation of redemption.

God Now Speaks Through His Son (vv. 2–4)

"Exact representation"

These words are the translation of the Greek word *charakter*. It means "impression, stamp." It refers to an engraved character or impress made by a die or a seal. It also indicates the characteristic trait or distinctive mark. It was used with special reference to any distinguishing peculiarity and, hence, indicated an exact reproduction. (Taken from Fritz Rienecker, *Linguistic Key to the Greek New Testament* [Grand Rapids: Zondervan, 1980], 664.)

Now, however, "in these last days" God "has spoken to us by a Son, whom he appointed heir of all things, through whom he also created the worlds" (v. 2, NRSV).

No longer must God's message be relayed through the prophets. It now comes directly through the Son, who is "the exact representation of his being, sustaining all things by his powerful word" (v. 3). This verse reminds the reader of John's insight that "through him all things were made; without him nothing was made that has been made" (John 1:3), and of Paul's profound word that "in him all things hold together" (Col. 1:17). It is in Christ that all the galaxies of the universe and every last atomic particle in all creation hold together.

As the writer asserted that Christ is superior to the Old Testament prophets, he made seven descriptive statements about Christ:

- He is the Son of God.
- He is the Heir of the universe.
- He is the Creator.
- He is the Radiance of divine glory.
- He is the Sustainer of the universe.
- He is the Redeemer from sin.
- He is the Exalted One.

These statements effectively drive home the writer's point that Christ is God's final and most complete message to human beings.

When the Son finished His redemptive work on earth, He sat down "at the right hand of the Majesty in heaven" (v. 3). As a result, He "became as much superior to angels as the name he has inherited is more superior to theirs" (v. 4). Christians are redeemed by a mighty Savior whose name is above every name. Seldom do we see so much "heavy" doctrine compressed into so few verses. These four verses have been called by some the most beautiful passage in the New Testament.

In the wake of these inspired words, the author of Hebrews has stirred the imagination of his readers. He has rooted them in their spiritual heritage, reminded them of their cleansing, and pointed them to their destiny.

■ *The Hebrew prophets had been God's spokes-*
■ *men who uniquely brought the word to His*
■ *chosen people. No longer now must God's*
■ *message be relayed through the prophets. It*
■ *now comes directly through the Son, who is*
■ *"the exact representation of his being, sus-*
■ *taining all things by his powerful word"*
■ *(1:3).*

JESUS IS SUPERIOR TO THE ANGELS (1:5–14)

The writer first declared that Jesus is superior to the angels and that His name is more excellent than theirs (v. 4). Next he focused on the witness of the Scriptures in support of that declaration. For the most part, the writer drew his quotes from the Septuagint.

Psalm 2:7 and 2 Samuel 7:14. Quoting from the Septuagint, the Greek translation of Psalm 2:7

The Septuagint

The Septuagint is the oldest Greek translation of the Hebrew Old Testament. It contains several apocryphal books. Most New Testament quotations of the Old Testament are from the Septuagint.

and 2 Samuel 7:14, he stated that the superiority of Jesus Christ to angels is demonstrated by the fact that of none of the angels did God ever say, "You are my Son; today I have become your Father," or, "I will be his Father, and he will be my Son" (v. 5).

Deuteronomy 32:43 and Psalms 97:7; 104:4. Later, when God "brings the firstborn into the world" (v. 6), the Scriptures (Deut. 32:43 and Ps. 97:7) demand, "Let all God's angels worship him" (v. 6). Then, referring to the angels as messengers, note the witness of Psalm 104:4: "He makes his angels winds, his servants flames of fire" (v. 7).

Psalm 45:6–7. The writer of Hebrews quoted Psalm 45:6–7 to magnify God's moral uprightness: "a scepter of justice will be the scepter of your kingdom. You love righteousness and hate wickedness" and to demonstrate how God anointed the Son "with the oil of joy" above His companions (vv. 8–9).

Psalms 102:25–27; 110:1. The writer of Hebrews quoted from Psalm 102:25–27 and Psalm 110:1 to illustrate God's permanence and the Son's exaltation at God's "right hand," together with His ultimate victory over all His spiritual and moral enemies (vv. 10–13).

The angels, according to the Scriptures, are "ministering spirits sent to serve those who will inherit salvation" (v. 14).

- *The writer of Hebrews brought to bear the*
- *witness of the Scriptures in support of the*
- *declaration that Jesus is superior to the*
- *angels. He used several Old Testament pas-*
- *sages to demonstrate Christ's superiority.*

QUESTIONS TO GUIDE YOUR STUDY

1. Before Christ came, what was the role of the prophets?
2. Why is Christ superior to the prophets?
3. The writer made seven statements regarding Christ. What point do these statements collectively make?
4. From the writer's use of the Old Testament, what do we learn about Christ's superiority to the angels?

"Drift away"

The Greek verb for *drift away* is used only this one time in the New Testament. Xenephon used it of a river flowing by. B. F. Westcott said it's a picture "of being swept along past the sure anchorage which is within reach." (A.T. Robertson, *Word Pictures in the New Testament*, vol. 5, 342.)

Verse 3 contains one of the great texts of the Bible, "How shall we escape if we ignore such a great salvation?" While this text, in recent times, has most often been used as an evangelistic call to commit one's life to Christ, it is actually a word directly addressed to Christians. Read in this light, it calls believers to moral alertness and spiritual watchfulness. It warns against laziness. It reminds believers not to ignore the salvation God has given, is giving, and will give to those who trust and obey Him.

The writer of Hebrews presented his first exhortation to remain faithful to Christ (vv. 1–4). If the giving of the Law in the Old Testament led its violators to be punished, how much greater will be the punishment for those who neglect the great salvation in Christ.

In the second part of this chapter, the writer discussed the incarnation, which resulted in two benefits for believers: (1) The death and Resurrection of Jesus made it possible for all believers to overcome the fear of death (vv. 14–15). (2) Because the incarnate Christ suffered and overcame temptation, He is able to help believers when they are tempted (v. 18).

A WARNING AGAINST NEGLECTING CHRIST (2:1–3)

The writer warned his readers that in the light of all God's redemptive activity, His angelic messengers, and what He had communicated through His Son, they need to pay close attention. God communicated a message that is a matter of life and death. If they really understand this, they won't drift away (v. 1).

At this point the writer used a how-much-more argument. He reminded his readers that when angels delivered God's message and it was not obeyed, those who failed to listen received the punishment they deserved. If this were true of a message delivered by angels, *how much more* would it be true of a message delivered by God's Son (v. 2).

This great salvation "was first announced by the Lord" (v. 3), Jesus Christ. He declared the good news by:

- His preaching
- His teaching
- His good works
- His virgin birth
- His sinless life
- His personal example
- His sacrificial death
- His powerful Resurrection

The readers of this letter were not personal witnesses of what Jesus did and taught. But they had been instructed by those who had been with Jesus. Moreover, the testimony concerning Jesus had been confirmed to these Christians by the Holy Spirit. This confirmation came through:

- Signs and wonders
- Variety of miracles
- Gifts of the Holy Spirit

SO GREAT SALVATION (2:4)

For the sake of convenience, salvation can be viewed from the two perspectives of Christ's saving work and the believer's experience of salvation. Christ's saving work involves already completed, ongoing, and future saving activity. The apex of Christ's completed work is His sacrificial death: Christ came to "give his life as a ransom for many" (Mark 10:45); Christ "entered once for all into the Holy Place. . . . with his own blood, thus obtaining eternal redemption" (Heb. 9:12, NRSV); "in Christ God was reconciling the world to himself, not counting their trespasses against them" (2 Cor. 5:19, NRSV). Here *ransom, redemption,* and *reconciliation* are synonyms for salvation. With reference to Christ's atoning work, the believer can confess, "I was saved when Jesus died for me."

Christ's present saving work primarily concerns Christ's role as Mediator (Rom. 8:34; Heb. 7:25; 1 John 2:1). Christ's future saving work chiefly concerns Christ's coming again "to bring salvation to those who eagerly await him" (Heb. 9:28, REB) and salvation from the wrath of God's final judgment (Rom. 5:9–10). Though Christ's sacrificial death is central, Christ's saving activity extends to the whole of His life, including His birth (Gal. 4:4–5), Resurrection (Rom. 4:25; 1 Cor. 15:17), and Ascension (Rom. 8:34).

The believer's experience also offers a perspective for viewing salvation. The experience again embraces the past, present, and future. God's initial work in the believer's life breaks down into various scenes: conviction of sin (John 16:8); repentance (turning) from sin to God (Luke 15:7, 10; 2 Cor. 7:10); faith which involves commitment of one's whole life to Christ (John 3:16, 36); and confession of Christ as Lord (Acts 2:21; Rom. 10:9–10). Scripture uses a wealth of images to describe this act: *new birth* (John 3:3; Titus 3:5); *new creation* (2 Cor. 5:17); *adoption* (Rom. 8:15; Gal. 4:4–5; Eph. 1:5); *empowerment to be God's children* (John 1:12); *the status of "saints"* (1 Cor. 1:2; 2 Cor. 1:1). This initial work in the believer's life is often termed *justification.* Justification, however, also embraces God's final judgment (Rom. 2:13; 3:20, 30).

God's ongoing work in the believer's life concerns the process of maturing in Christ (Heb. 2:3; 1 Pet. 2:2), growing in Christ's service (Eph. 4:15; 2 Pet. 3:18), and experiencing victory over sin through the power of the Holy Spirit (Rom. 7–8). Here sin remains a reality in the believer's life (Rom. 7; 1 John 1:8–2:1). The believer is caught in between what God has begun and what God is yet to complete (Phil. 1:6; 2:12).

God's yet-to-be-finished work in the lives of all believers is sometimes called *glorification* (Rom. 8:17; Heb. 2:10). Scripture, however, uses a wealth of terms for this future saving work: *adoption* (Rom. 8:23); *redemption* (Luke 21:28; Rom. 8:23; Eph. 4:30); *salvation* (Rom. 13:11; Heb. 1:14; 9:28; 1 Pet. 1:5; 2:2); and *sanctification* (1 Thess. 5:23). God's future work involves more than the individual; God's future work extends to the renewal of heaven and earth.

■ *The writer presented his first exhortation to*
■ *his readers to remain faithful to Christ and*
■ *warned them against ignoring Him. The*
■ *superiority of Christ makes the failure to*
■ *believe on Him a feared experience.*

THE VALUE OF CHRIST'S INCARNATION (2:5–13)

The World Is Subjected to the Crucified Lord (vv. 5–9)

God hasn't put angels in charge of the world to come. God's intent is to give human beings dominion in the world to come. Here the writer quoted Psalm 8.

It has been claimed that the Dead Sea Scrolls show the sectarians of Qumran believed that the coming Age would be marked by the dominion of Michael and his angelic subordinates.

The writer observed that the world is not yet subject to human beings. He interprets Psalm 8 as applying to the world to come.

While we don't see the present world subject to man, we see Jesus who, for a time, was made lower than the angels. The Son became human so that He might suffer and taste death for everyone. God's love of and grace toward sinful

"Taste death"

"The phrase to taste death occurs in the gospels (Matt. 16:28; Mark 9:1; Luke 9:27; John 8:52), though not in ancient Greek. It means to see death (Heb. 11:5), a bitter experience, not a rapid sip (Moffatt). The death of Christ (Andrew Fuller) was sufficient for all, efficient for some." (A.T. Robertson, *Word Pictures in the New Testament*, vol. 5, 346.)

human beings led the Son to be made lower than the angels for the purpose of fully tasting death for everyone.

Jesus Is the Author of Our Salvation (vv. 10–13)

As the "Author" of our salvation, the Son has been made "perfect through suffering" (v. 10). The word *author* here may be translated "leader," "originator," or "trailblazer." He didn't need to be made perfect or complete because He was sinful. He entered time and became subject to the processes of time so that He might bring with Him many sons to glory.

The writer of Hebrews went on to explain that because of the Incarnation, believers become part of God's spiritual family. As God is our Father, so Jesus is our Elder Brother. He is not ashamed to identify with us as members of His own family. In God's gracious providence, we are His kin. Christ who sets Christians apart in salvation and authentic holiness of life and the ones who are so set apart have the same source.

God emptied Himself in the Incarnation (Phil. 2:6–8) at which time He became fully human. When that happened, humanity found its name in the man Jesus Christ (vv. 12–13).

■ *The author concluded that Christ's Incarna-*
■ *tion and Crucifixion enhance His superiority*
■ *and qualify Him to become a spiritual trail-*
■ *blazer for believers; that is, the Author of*
■ *their salvation.*

RESULTS OF THE INCARNATION
(2:14–18)

Christians Are No Longer Enslaved to Death (vv. 14–15)

Jesus shared our nature to the extent that He became subject to death. His tasting death had the result of destroying the devil, the one who has the power of death. In doing so, He liberates human beings who have been enslaved by the fear of death all of their lives.

Adam and Eve disobeyed God and ate the forbidden fruit of which God had said, "For when you eat of it you will surely die" (Gen. 2:17). The moment they willfully disobeyed Him, they began to die; and the human race has been dying ever since. Because of man's fallen and sinful condition, he is enslaved to death—his last, great enemy. However, Jesus conquered this last great enemy in the Resurrection. His Resurrection took the sting out of death and the victory out of the grave, and now death is swallowed up in life (v. 15).

As Christians, our roots are established fully and firmly in God's Son, the Author of our great salvation and the Source of our entire being. Our fruits are nurtured by God's indwelling Spirit, who is the source of the believer's productivity. If we are rightly rooted in the source, fruit bearing will appropriately come. If we are truly fruitful, it is because our life and work have Him as our spiritual source.

Jesus Helps Us Overcome Temptation (vv. 16–18)

The writer revealed a second great benefit of the Incarnation for believers. Jesus identified not with angels (v. 16) but with us "so that he might become a merciful and faithful high priest in the service of God, to make expiation for the sins of the people" (v. 17, RSV).

In the Jewish system, the sins of the people were forgiven as the priests made prescribed sacrifices on behalf of sinners. Atonement of some kind is at the heart of every religion. That is, religion universally offers some way for sinners to get rid of their sin. In most religious systems, human acts are required to banish sin and bridge the

Make an inventory of some of your fears. Notice how each of those fears is related to the fear of death. There is an inverse relationship between fear of death and enjoyment of life. The less fear of death, the greater the capacity to live—even in this world.

Because Jesus Christ knows human life personally, with its suffering and temptation, "he is able to help those who are tempted" (v. 18). In what ways have you been tempted recently? Being tempted is not a sin. Jesus was sinless, yet He knew temptation better than any human being. Next time you are tempted remember Jesus.

"He himself suffered"

The tense of the verb *suffer* (the Greek *perfect* tense) is important in understanding the impact of this statement. "The perfect tense serves to emphasize that, though the temptation Christ suffered in the flesh is a thing of the past, yet its effect is permanent, the effect of compassion and understanding as He aids us in the hour of our temptation." (Fritz Rienecker, *Linguistic Key to the Greek New Testament* [Grand Rapids: Zondervan, 1980], 671.)

chasm between humanity and deity. In Christianity, however, it is Jesus Christ Himself, the "faithful high priest," whose divine act of self-sacrifice on the Cross has banished our sin and bridged the gap. He is our Bridge Man.

The Author of our salvation is our trailblazer to glory. The writer simply stated that "he is able" (v. 18). What an incomparable affirmation about our Lord and Savior!

■ *Christ's Incarnation gives believers two ben-*
■ *efits. First, the death and Resurrection of*
■ *Jesus make it possible for all believers to*
■ *overcome the fear of death. Second, because*
■ *the incarnate Christ suffered and overcame*
■ *temptation, He is able to help believers when*
■ *they are tempted.*

QUESTIONS TO GUIDE YOUR STUDY

1. What is the content of the writer's warning in Hebrews 2:1–4?
2. How would you define *salvation*? What does it entail? How is it made possible?
3. One of the believer's benefits of the Incarnation is that Christians must no longer fear death. How did Jesus accomplish this?
4. A second benefit of the Incarnation is that Christ is able to aid us in our temptation. What has qualified Him to do so?

In this chapter the author contrasted Moses with Christ and clearly proved the superiority of Christ over Moses and his ministry. He also mentioned the unbelief shown by the Jewish generations in the time of Moses and warned his readers not to follow their evil example.

In comparing Jesus to Moses, the writer pointed out that Moses was a servant of God *in* God's house, that is, among the people of God. In contrast, however, Jesus was God's Son, serving *over* that house. The superiority of Jesus' position is obvious (vv. 5–6).

Joshua led the Jews of his generation to rest in Canaan. Jesus, however, brought the people of God into a resting place that provided eternal spiritual benefits (4:1–10). The superiority of the destination provided by Jesus is again obvious.

The writer was aware that a crisis faced his readers just as the Jews in the lifetime of Moses and Joshua confronted crises. He warned that unbelief could prevent them from entering a relationship of promise just as it had in an earlier generation. The problem earlier was unbelief (3:18; 4:11), and he wanted his readers to avoid the spiritual defeat caused by unbelief.

THE SUPERIORITY OF JESUS TO MOSES (3:1–6)

Because of Christ's superiority in providing salvation to those who are willing to receive it, Christians are to consider Jesus further (v. 1). The writer, for the first time, addressed and identified the first recipients of this letter. The writer called them "holy brothers." That is, they

The Superiority of Christ's Work in Hebrews

Work	Passage	Result
1. Priesthood	4:14–7:28	He pointed to the superior priesthood of Christ.
2. Covenant	8:1–13	He explained the superior covenant Christ founded in relationship to human beings.
3. Sacrifice	9:1–10:18	He described the superior sacrifice Christ offered for our redemption.

This is a powerful reminder that the church must never draw its net of evangelism so loosely and so irresponsibly as to count its membership as anything other than a holy brotherhood closely related to our holy God. A Christian's relationship to Him should show up in every relationship and circumstance.

are brothers and sisters together with the writer in the family of God, and they are "holy" in the sense that they are separated to God in their life and conduct.

Christians share in a "heavenly calling" (v. 1). All believers have a gift. Some are chosen for one office and some for another, but God has called from heaven to come to life and light through the gospel. The writer urged his readers to "fix your thoughts on Jesus, the apostle and high priest whom we confess." This is a unique challenge. Nowhere else in the Bible do we find one that compares precisely to it. To fix one's thoughts on Jesus is to observe Him so as to understand His profound significance. It is an effort to perceive Him in all His fullness, concentrating on the true meaning of His life and work.

Jesus the Apostle. As "the apostle," Jesus is God's special Messenger and authoritative Spokesman concerning His New Covenant of grace made with His believing and behaving people.

Jesus the High Priest. As the "high priest," He is the One who enables and mediates our confession. As God's special Apostle, Jesus has come from God to us; and as High Priest, He has gone to God for us. He has done, once for all, the work of going between "the Judge of all the earth" (Gen. 18:25) and us. Our confession, as Christians, is that Jesus Christ, God's apostle and our High Priest, is our Lord. No formula, no creed, no set of doctrines, no human document can ever be the proper object of the believer's confession. We confess Christ. With our minds and hearts we believe and are justified (Rom. 10:10), and with our lives and mouths we confess and are saved.

Fixing Our Thoughts on Jesus

His Role	His Ministry
Apostle	God's special messenger and spokesman concerning His new covenant of grace.
High Priest	The One who enables and mediates our confession before God.

We are to fix our thoughts on Jesus because of His faithfulness (v. 2). Jesus was "faithful" to the Father "who appointed him" or commissioned him as Moses had been "faithful in all God's house" (v. 2). This reference to Moses picks up the statement attributed to the Lord in Numbers 12:7 and acknowledges the special respect or even veneration paid by the Jews to Moses, their great deliverer from Egyptian bondage. The house of God is God's entire household or family, and this term is meant to include all God's redeemed people delivered from the bondage of sin by His grace.

Jesus is more worthy of glory than Moses, just as the builder of a house is worthy of more honor than the house he has built (v. 3). "The builder of everything," it is observed parenthetically, is

God (v. 4). Moses was faithful as a steward, "but Christ is faithful as a son" (vv. 5–6).

The writer sounded a word of caution to keep his readers from turning aside from their commitment to God: "We are his house, if we hold on to our courage and hope of which we boast" (v. 6). Christians have always been prone to relax in their spiritual discipline, to drift, to grow lukewarm, and even to let go of their first love. This word is an antidote for the poison of such carelessness. Believers are the family in God's own household if they hold fast to him as He holds fast to them. If we proudly hold to our hope in Him, remaining steadfast to the end, He will surely provide His loving care and never-failing protection.

■ *Christ was God's Son who reigned over the*
■ *household of God's people. He was superior*
■ *to Moses, who was merely a servant within*
■ *God's household. Moses was faithful as a*
■ *steward, but Christ is faithful as a Son.*

A WARNING AGAINST UNBELIEF (3:7–19)

Hebrews 3:7–11 is a quotation of Psalm 95:7–11. The preacher of Hebrews loved the Bible. He quoted it freely and at length. He skillfully appropriated it to make some of his important points. Here he called it to mind with special attribution, "As the Holy Spirit says" (v. 7). It was God's Spirit who warned the Jews in the psalmist's time, and it is his Spirit who warns Christians in our own time not to harden their hearts in rebellion (vv. 7–11).

The author of Hebrews appropriately used this psalm to remind his readers to keep on hearing God's voice, to keep on walking in God's ways, and to keep on holding fast to the hope of entering into God's eternal rest, which He is preparing for His faithful people. The psalmist here linked together two dramatic events from Israel's Exodus from Egypt: (1) their murmuring anxiety over the apparent lack of water in the wilderness; and (2) the pessimistic report of the apprehensive spies who caused the people to shrink back from the immediate conquest of the Promised Land that God intended. Both incidents illustrate their lack of faith. This passage in Hebrews deals with that same kind of complaining and fearful unbelief in the lives of Christians today.

"See to it" (v. 12) is a solemn warning. Caution in the presence of aggressive evil is appropriate. Humility is in order. Those who think they are standing must be careful that they don't fall (1 Cor. 10:12). The writer issued this particularly forceful warning so that none of his readers "has a sinful, unbelieving heart that turns away from the living God" (v. 12). He urged his Christian "brothers" to take care to avoid the fate of those who wandered in the wilderness for forty years and died because they would not put their faith to work.

When the heart harbors unbelief, that unbelief leads to:

- separation from God by giving way to "sin's deceitfulness" (vv. 12–13).
- hardness of heart and rebellion (v. 15).
- disobedience (v. 18).
- inability to enter into God's rest (v. 19).

The Cycle of Unbelief

Step	Progression	Result
Unbelief	leads to →	Disobedience
Disobedience	issues in →	Sin
Sin	brings on →	Punishment

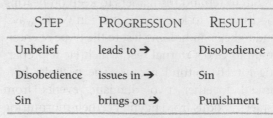

The writer advised his readers to "encourage one another daily" (v. 13). It is a part of our continuing responsibility as Christians to prop up one another. In the community of obedient and active faith, believers are to cultivate an everlastingly vigilant concern for one another. Such daily encouragement helps the family of believers to avoid the deceitfulness of sin. The mutual admonishment of believers involves the sharing of the warnings and cautions, affirmations and encouragements, and the edification and nourishment that are required for Christians to grow in the grace and the knowledge of Christ. For this to take place effectively, it is imperative that God's people be steeped in God's Word.

God's oath of exclusion (v. 11) is a solemn warning for us to bear in mind against the great Judgment Day.

The writer reminded his audience that "today" (v. 15) is the time when opportunity is still knocking, when hope is still beckoning, when God is still speaking, and when the Spirit is still calling. He will not be stopped short of calling believers to hold firmly to their original confidence in Christ and to maintain steadfast commitment to Him (v. 14). His point is that we keep on enjoying Christ as we keep on enduring. We keep on being delivered from disobedience, rebellion, callousness of spirit, sin, and death as we keep on believing. Though the unbelieving Hebrew children "were not able to enter" the Promised Land "because of their unbelief" (v. 19), we who maintain our faith and endure to the end are assured of entering God's rest.

This chapter begins with a compelling presentation of Jesus' superiority and ends with a ringing challenge for Christians to endure.

- *The writer warns his readers not to harden*
- *their hearts in rebellion as did the Israelites*
- *in the wilderness wandering. Jesus' superi-*
- *ority to Moses makes it a more serious mat-*
- *ter to reject Jesus than to reject Moses.*
- *Unbelieving people will not enter into God's*
- *heavenly rest.*

QUESTIONS TO GUIDE YOUR STUDY

1. Why is Christ superior to Moses?
2. How does Jesus function as both an *apostle* and our *High Priest*?
3. The writer warned his readers of unbelief. Why was he so concerned? What would be the result of their unbelief?
4. The writer advised his readers to "encourage one another daily." What are some ways Christians can do this?

Joshua led the Jews of his generation to rest in Canaan. Jesus, however, brings the people of God into a resting place that provides eternal, spiritual benefits. The superiority of what Jesus provides is again obvious.

The writer was aware that his readers face a crisis just as the Jews in the lifetime of Moses and Joshua confronted crises. He warned that unbelief could prevent them from entering a relationship of promise just as it had in an earlier generation. As expressed in chapter 3, the writer of Hebrews wanted his readers to avoid the spiritual defeat caused by unbelief.

THE SUPERIORITY OF JESUS TO JOSHUA (4:1–8)

A Caution Against Missing God's Rest (vv. 1–2)

"God's rest"

The word *rest* is a compound word made up of the preposition *down* and the word *cease*. It refers to a "causing to cease" or "putting to rest" (Acts 7:49; Heb. 3:11; 4:8). It refers primarily to the rest in Canaan and then the heavenly rest in which God dwells. (See A. T. Robertson, *Word Pictures in the New Testament*, "The Epistle to the Hebrews," vol. 5, 357.)

The writer called Christians to moral alertness. God's offer of rest is open. They need to press on and not fall short of the promised rest (v. 1).

He admonished his readers to "be careful." One of the aids to pressing on is to cultivate a healthy fear of the awful consequences of failing to reach God's rest. Again, the pastoral concern of the author of Hebrews is coming through loud and clear. This is the concern of the church, God's caring community. The phrase "the promise . . . still stands" reminds us of the attention the book of Hebrews gives to the promises of God.

As good news came from Moses to the Israelites during their bondage in Egypt, so through Jesus Christ the Good News has been "preached to us" (v. 2) while we were in bondage to sin. The message they heard from Moses did not benefit them because it was not met with personal faith on their part (v. 2). Recalling the Israelites' example, the writer urged Christians to hear with faith the Good News that had been proclaimed to them.

The Scope of God's Rest (vv. 3–8)

In these verses the writer mentioned three kinds of rest:

- God's resting from His work on the seventh day of Creation.
- The rest of God's people in Canaan.
- The eternal rest of God's people.

Many, through unbelief, refused to enter the rest in Canaan when Joshua lead the Israelites. Even those who entered the rest in Canaan found that this was not a permanent rest.

God has made provision for an eternal rest for His people. Jesus is the leader who opens the way for this rest. On the human side, faith is the condition that enables persons to enter this rest. This rest is both present and future. Believers begin to experience this rest now and will experience this eternal rest in its fullness in the world to come.

God's rest has been ready from the beginning. No works on the part of the Creator-Redeemer remain to be done, for "on the seventh day God rested from all his work" (v. 4). His rest was denied to the disobedient Hebrew children (v. 5); "it still remains that some will enter that rest" who choose to turn to God through faith in Jesus Christ (v. 6). He has set today as the "certain day" of salvation (v. 7). Even Joshua was not able to deliver rest to God's people (v. 8).

■ *The writer shows that Joshua failed to lead*
■ *the people of God to rest because of their*
■ *unbelief. However, those who have received*
■ *the gospel of Christ may enter that rest. Sal-*
■ *vation is an accomplished fact. Those who*
■ *make the commitment to Christ enter God's*
■ *rest without delay.*

THE URGENCY OF SEEKING GOD'S REST (4:9–13)

A time will come when the blessed repose and perfect peace that God has promised Christians will be theirs: "There remains . . . a Sabbath-rest for the people of God" (v. 9).

This passage is a thumbnail sketch of the interaction between God and humankind in history. The writer of this letter issued yet another strong challenge to his readers: "Let us, therefore, strive to enter that rest, that no one fall by the same sort of disobedience" (v. 11).

God's people need not stumble in disobedience, drift in disbelief, or fall away in apostasy. Here the writer brought the strongest imaginable antidote to taking a destructive path: the Word of God.

God's Word is alive and active. It is exceedingly sharp and able to probe and discern the contents of the human heart. In fact, nothing in the human heart is able to escape the gaze of God.

Sinners love darkness rather than light because their deeds are evil (John 3:19). Like Adam and Eve, attempting to hide from God after their rebellious disobedience, sinful humans seek to avoid God's sight. The writer called his readers

"Let us strive"

This exhortation contains an interesting contrast: "strive" and "enter rest." Diligent activity, effort, exertion, work precede the entry into the rest God has promised.

"This is the judgment, that the Light has come into the world, and men loved the darkness rather than the Light, for their deeds were evil. For everyone who does evil hates the Light, and does not come to the Light, for fear that his deeds will be exposed. But he who practices the truth comes to the Light, so that his deeds may be manifested as having been wrought in God" (John 3:19–21, NASB).

to realize that every day and every moment God sees every act, hears every word, knows every motive, numbers every heartbeat, and counts every hair. As we—open to the gaze of God—realize all we are and all God wants to be and do for us, we will stay on course to the rest God has for us.

■ *The writer issued yet another strong chal-*
■ *lenge to his readers: "Let us, therefore, make*
■ *every effort to enter that rest, so that no one*
■ *will fall by following their example of disobe-*
■ *dience" (v. 11). Jesus promised rest to His*
■ *people if they believe and follow the promises*
■ *of the gospel.*

CHRISTIAN CONFESSION TO BE HELD LAST (4:14–16)

The writer further encouraged faithfulness on the part of believers by reminding them that they have a great high priest who has entered heaven on their behalf. As the high priest on earth entered the holy of holies, so Jesus has entered the heavens on our behalf. With that in view, the writer urged his readers to hold fast to their profession of faith.

Consider further the character of our great High Priest.

He is sympathetic with our weaknesses. Although he is God's Son, when He took on human flesh, He came to know firsthand what it was to live as a human being in a fallen world. He also came to know what it is like to be tempted. In every case He resisted the temptation and was completely without sin.

High Priest

The high priest was the priest in charge of the Temple worship. In the Levitical priesthood, the high priest went once each year, on the great Day of Atonement, through the curtain into the Holy of Holies, the innermost and holiest place, to make special sacrifice for his own sins and for the sins of all the people. Sprinkling the blood of the sin offering seven times before and on the mercy seat, he symbolically covered the sins of the people from the eyes of the Lord. Now Jesus, our great High Priest, has passed, once for all, not through the inner curtain of a tabernacle made with human hands, but "through the heavens" (v. 14) to God Himself to make atonement for all our sins.

"Hold fast"

"Here the writer is urging believers to cling tenaciously to their confession of Christ. Cling now and keep on clinging." (A. T. Robertson, *Word Pictures in the New Testament*, "The Epistle to the Hebrews," vol.5, 365.)

"Throne of grace"

The "throne of grace" (v. 16) speaks both of God's sovereignty and of His compassion. As King of kings, he is enthroned by His very nature. His throne, however, is not one from which harsh and capricious judgments are thundered out. Rulings from God's throne are never arbitrary, never prejudiced, never biased, never merciless. On the contrary, those rulings are gracious. The presence of God is here characterized as "the throne of grace." Nowhere else in the entire Bible does this beautiful description appear. Yet this concept is universally known and generally used throughout Christendom because it uniquely draws together vitally important insights about the nature and character of God.

In light of these truths, God's people can "approach the throne of grace with confidence," so they may receive mercy and find grace to help in their time of need (v. 16). This text is another of those brilliant gems from the treasure box of Hebrews. The writer of Hebrews was tender and pastoral here. God opened His heart of grace and love to us. It is now possible for us to approach Him.

In Jesus Christ, God has shown us His face. In Jesus Christ, God has bared to us His heart. In His loving presence, we "receive mercy and find grace to help us in our time of need" (v. 16). Our "time of need" is always. Thank God for His grace which supplies every need we have according to His riches in glory through Christ Jesus (Phil. 4:19). He is ever eager to supply our need. Let us then approach Him with confidence.

- *Christ is our great High Priest who represents us in God's presence. Because His sacrifice made atonement for all our sins, salvation may be appropriated by anyone who wants it. Therefore, God's people can "approach the throne of grace with confidence" to receive mercy and find grace to help in their time of need.*

QUESTIONS TO GUIDE YOUR STUDY

1. Why is Jesus superior to Joshua?
2. What is "God's rest"? What did it mean to the Israelites wandering in the desert? What is its significance to believers in Christ?

3. Why is it urgent for believers to seek God's rest?

4. The writer explained that Christians have in Jesus a High Priest. What does that mean to the believer in Christ?

The most frequent use of *grace* in Old Testament times had to do with finding favor in the sight of God or some human authority like an earthly ruler. Now, through Christ, all believers may approach God and find His unmerited favor. He is not willing that any should perish but that all should come to life. "I take no pleasure in the death of anyone, declares the Sovereign Lord. Repent and live!" (Ezek. 18:32). In Christ we come to the throne of grace, respond to this prophetic call to turn or to repent, and receive from God His great gift of life eternal and life abundant.

The High Priest's Offering for Sin

Under special appointment from God "every high priest is selected from among men and is appointed to represent them in matters relating to God, to offer gifts and sacrifices for sins" (v. 1). Sins cannot be taken lightly. The high priest's offering was not merely a bit of impressive ritual perfunctorily done. It was "for sins" of rebellion against God, of willful disobedience, of intentional mark missing, of perversity, of transgression, of trespasses, of evil, of violence, of injustice, of unrighteousness. A righteous God dealing with a morally responsible human race requires that sin be taken seriously and that it be dealt with seriously.

In this chapter the writer outlined two similarities between Christ as High Priest and the priests after Aaron. Both showed the ability to understand sympathetically the needs of human beings before God, and both were called by God to carry out their work.

In this passage the writer issued his most serious warning against committing apostasy and turning away from Christ. He urged them to move beyond spiritual infancy into maturity, a theme he continued in the next chapter.

THE COMPARISON OF CHRIST AND AARON (5:1–4)

The statement in 4:15–16 declared that as believers hold on to their confession, they may confidently approach God's throne of grace. Through the special ministry of Jesus Christ, the great High Priest, they may receive mercy and find grace to help in time of need.

Called by God (vv. 1–3)

The writer informed us that "every high priest is selected from among men and is appointed to represent them in matters related to God, to offer gifts and sacrifices for sins" (v. 1). The high priest does not take the office on his own initiative, nor is he elected by the people. God established the office, and the person occupying the office "must be called by God, just as Aaron was" (v. 4). Nor does he "take upon himself the glory of becoming a high priest" (v. 5).

The high priest under the Levitical system could "deal gently with those who are ignorant and are going astray, since he himself is subject to weakness. This is why he has to offer sacrifices for his own sins, as well as for the sins of the people" (vv. 2–3).

Aaron's Priesthood (v. 4)

To be especially chosen, appointed, or ordained is to be entrusted with special responsibility by the one choosing, appointing, or ordaining. The writer mentioned Aaron because the priestly line began with him. Aaron served with prominence and distinction as the first one to be particularly consecrated or set apart for what God called His priesthood (Exod. 28:1–3).

THE PRIESTHOOD OF CHRIST (5:5–10)

Jesus Christ, our great High Priest under God's New Covenant, also was called by the Father. Nor did He exalt Himself to do the high priestly work. The Father exalted Him (v. 5). His special ordination from God was, "You are a priest forever, in the order of Melchizedek" (v. 6). This is the first reference in Hebrews to Melchizedek, but eight other references in the letter to the Hebrews follow (chaps. 5–7).

Melchizedek

Who was Melchizedek? Genesis 14:18 identifies him as "king of Salem" and as the priest of "God Most High." To him Abraham, the father of the faithful, gave tithes (Gen. 14:20).

The name *Melchizedek* means "Zedek is my king" or "my king is righteousness." He was a priest and king of Salem, a city identified with Jerusalem.

Old Testament. When Abraham returned from the Valley of Siddim where he defeated Chedorlaomer, king of Elam, and the kings aligned with Chedorlaomer, Melchizedek greeted Abraham with bread and wine. He blessed Abraham in the name of "God Most High." In return, Abraham gave Melchizedek a tenth of everything. Melchizedek and Abraham both worshiped the one true God. Abraham also appeared to recognize the role of Melchizedek as a priest. Psalm 110:4 refers to one who would be forever a priest "in the order of Melchizedek."

This messianic psalm teaches that the leader or ruler of the Hebrew nation would be able to reflect in his person the role of priest as well as the role of king.

New Testament. The writer of Hebrews made several references in chapters 5–7 to Jesus' priesthood being of the "order of Melchizedek" as opposed to Levitical in nature. The author of Hebrews cited Psalm 110:4. For the writer of Hebrews, only Jesus, whose life could not be destroyed by death, fit the psalmist's description of a priest of the "order of Melchizedek."

Christ's Humanity. Combining the high priesthood of Aaron and the unique high priesthood of Melchizedek, Jesus prayed and made earnest supplication to God. In His complete identification with humanity, Jesus prayed as we pray. He petitioned God as we do. He cried aloud as we do in times of personal crisis. He wept as we sometimes do. As with all who truly trust God, Jesus "was heard because of his reverent submission" (v. 7).

Christ's Suffering. Although God's only begotten Son, Jesus "learned obedience from what he suffered" (v. 8), the creative pain of suffering taught Jesus obedience to the Father and subjection to His will.

Christ's Perfection. Jesus, "once made perfect . . . became the source of eternal salvation for all who obey him" (v. 9). The treasure chest of Hebrews is open again, and another priceless jewel is flashing here in verses 8–9. The *perfection* that Jesus achieved was accomplished through His death and Resurrection.

Christ's Obedience. God appointed Him, and He responded with absolute faith, complete obedience, and redemptive suffering. His obedience was not a conditioned response to external stimuli. It was rather a supremely moral, absolutely responsible response to the Father's leadership. Though Jesus was God's Son, His humanity was so total that He actually "learned" obedience through the things that He suffered along life's way, such painful experiences as the great temptation, Lazarus's death, Jerusalem's refusal to know the things that make for peace, the disciples' petty jealousies, Peter's denial, Pilate's harsh sentence, and the agony of Crucifixion.

■ *God appointed Aaron as a high priest to rep-*
■ *resent people before God. Because Aaron was*
■ *surrounded with weakness, he was able to*
■ *have compassion on other weak, sinful*
■ *people. Christ also faced hardship, and He*
■ *learned the value of obedience by His com-*
■ *mitment to God's will. He is the source of*
■ *eternal salvation for all those who obey Him.*

The eternal salvation which has Jesus as its source is given to "all who obey him" (v. 9). The divine imperative is for us to obey Him. There is no other way out of the dark valley of sin and death except the high and narrow way of obedience to Him.

COUNSEL TO KEEP MOVING TOWARD MATURITY (5:11–14)

The writer declared to his readers that they are "slow to learn" (v. 11). They had once heard the word of the gospel with keenly attentive ears. Familiarity with the good news, however, seems gradually to have hardened their hearing. "By this time" they ought to have so disciplined themselves in the faith and so developed in their own Christian experience that they could "be teachers" (v. 12), bringing others to the knowledge of Christ and obedience to Him in their daily lives.

The writer of Hebrews delivered a powerful moral meaning in this passage. He distinguished the mature adult from the immature child by the commitment to be morally responsible, to be morally discriminating, and to make consistently moral judgments. Christian maturity is related to the development of skill in the use of "the teaching about righteousness" (v. 13). This phrase is a reference to moral truth. It has to do with the "glue" that holds civilization together. Without "the teaching about righteousness" both religious institutions and civil structures would crumble and fall apart.

Certainly, without qualified and able teachers and serious teaching, any church is in deep trouble. Discipleship is at the heart of all authentic church life. Where there is no real learning, there can be no committed disciples.

The writer continued his chastisement: "You need milk, not solid food!" (v. 12). They ought to have been ashamed. They were behaving like babies, like immature children "not acquainted with the teaching about righteousness" (v. 13). He challenged his readers to realize that "solid food is for the mature, who by constant use have trained themselves to distinguish good from evil" (v. 14).

Formal teaching is valuable and has its place, but the real proof that the lesson has been truly learned is when it is put into practice. When we become disciplined to discern between good and evil, we then consistently choose the right and reject the wrong and move responsibly toward maturity in Christ.

Mature Christians "who by constant use have trained themselves to distinguish good from evil" (v. 14), have made the "teaching about righteousness" part of their lifestyle. Christians are not to abandon the basics but to build on them. A foundation is absolutely necessary, but it is no substitute for a superstructure.

■ *The writer declared to his readers that they*
■ *are "slow to learn." He challenged his read-*
■ *ers to become disciplined to discern between*
■ *good and evil, consistently to choose the right*
■ *and reject the wrong and move responsibly*
■ *toward maturity in Christ.*

QUESTIONS TO GUIDE YOUR STUDY

1. Why does the writer mention Aaron's priesthood?
2. Describe Christ's priesthood. How does it differ from the Aaronic priesthood?
3. What is the result of Christ's priesthood?
4. What is the "teaching about righteousness" the writer mentioned in verse 13?

"Constant use"

This word is also translated "practice" (v. 14, NRSV). It is the word for *habit*, referring to a habit of body or mind indicating not the process but the result. That is, the condition has been produced by past exercise and is then the habitual or normal condition, the disposition or character. (Taken from Fritz Rienecker, *Linguistic Key to the Greek New Testament* [Grand Rapids: Zondervan, 1980], 680.)

In this chapter the writer described his readers as immature and urged them to move beyond spiritual infancy into maturity (vv. 1–2). He warned that if they finally renounce Christ, they will forfeit all hope of eternal salvation (vv. 3–6). He also reminded his readers that they have borne fruit that demonstrates salvation, but he wanted them to avoid becoming lazy and careless in their Christian profession (vv. 7–12).

ELEMENTARY TEACHINGS (6:1–3)

The writer now challenged his readers to move on to maturity. Apparently they were stuck in laying the foundations of the Christian faith over and over again. The foundations are important, but they are designed to enable believers to grow in their faith.

THE ELEMENTARY TEACHINGS OF THE FAITH

- Repentance from acts that lead to death

- Faith in God

- Instruction about baptism

- Instruction about the laying on of hands

- The resurrection of the dead

- Eternal judgment

"Repentance from acts that lead to death" (v. 1)
Repentance is a keynote in the New Testament message. Its great prominence in the early church is reason enough for its being mentioned first in this passage. *Repentance* is godly sorrow for sin and an intentional turning away from sin.

For those who have trusted in works to make them right with God, repentance is necessary so that the work of the great High Priest, Jesus Christ, can take effect.

The phrase "acts that lead to death" does not refer to Hebrew ceremonialism but rather to those activities, interests, and pleasures that pertain to spiritual death. They are moral offenses from which a person must break away in order to become a Christian. Dead works are like a sheepskin over a wolf. One is still a wolf even though he or she may be in sheep's clothing. In conversion, Christians learn to trust Christ for new hearts while distrusting the former covering of dead works that once occupied their energies.

"Faith in God" (v. 1)

This is the saving faith that believers direct to the Lord when they first believe. It is closely connected to repentance. It is not merely the belief that there is a God or simply faith in His existence. It is a genuine trust in Him as Redeemer, Savior, and Lord.

"Instruction about baptisms" (v. 2)

This reference is not clear. Because it is part of a list of the elementary teachings of the Christian faith, it is better understood as singular ("baptism") instead of plural ("baptisms"). Some believe the reference is to immersions such as those practiced by some of the Jewish cults for initiates, proselytes, and regular gatherings of the faithful. Many ancient religions used all kinds of purification rites connected with water. The distinctively Christian use of water for believer's baptism, therefore, had to be carefully taught to early Christians, who needed to distinguish between similar rites practiced by non-Christians.

Instruction about "the laying on of hands" (v. 2)

This is the early church's recognition of special needs for the Holy Spirit's indwelling and empowering for Christian work. Ordination in any highly formal sense for a special class of ministers like preachers, teachers, deacons, or missionaries is apparently not intended here.

"The resurrection of the dead" (v. 2).

This is a crucial doctrine of Christian faith. It is vital that all believers understand this teaching and its significance early in the Christian life.

"Eternal judgment" (v. 2)

This is another vital doctrine the readers of this letter needed to understand, as do modern readers. Human beings do not die as animals, with no hope for eternity. On the contrary, all people will experience God's righteous judgment following death. Then, for eternity, each person will live with the choices he or she made in life.

The writer apparently did not intend to mention each and every elementary doctrine that Christians embrace. He drew out, under the Holy Spirit's leadership, these primary points with which his Christian converts would be familiar. Churches today would also do well to make sure every convert gains a working knowledge of these basic concepts.

Note that although the writer of Hebrews admonished believers to leave these elementary teachings, they are not to lose them. Instead, they are to build on them, add to them, and fulfill them. "And God permitting, we will do so" (v. 3), is a way of saying that forward movement in the Christian life is our doing by His mercy.

■ *The writer described his readers as imma-*
■ *ture and urged them to move beyond spiri-*
■ *tual infancy into maturity. He did not intend*
■ *that they abandon the basics but rather build*
■ *on them and add to them.*

PERSEVERANCE IN CHRIST (6:4–8)

Bringing One Back to Repentance (vv. 4–6)

These three verses are among the most solemn and most discussed in all the Scriptures. A key word in these verses is *impossible*.

What is impossible? It is impossible to bring some people back to repentance.

Who are these people?

- They have been brought to the light.
- They have tasted of the heavenly gift.
- They have shared in the Holy Spirit.
- They have known firsthand how good God's Word is.
- They have experienced the powers of the world to come.

Under what conditions is it impossible to bring such persons back to repentance? If they fall away. A person who falls away continues to crucify the Son of God and hold Him in contempt.

A key question in interpreting this passage is whether the people described above have been saved. Some take the position that in spite of all they have experienced they haven't been saved. Salvation is from first to last a work of God that cannot be reversed by human beings.

Some interpret the falling away as a hypothetical possibility that can't happen in reality.

"Fall away"

John Calvin noted that a lot is at stake in our understanding what the writer meant here by *fall away*: "Whoever then understands its meaning, can easily extricate himself from every difficulty. But it must be noticed, that there is a twofold falling away, one particular, and the other general. He who has in anything, or in anyway offended, has fallen away from his state as a Christian; therefore all sins are so many fallings. But the Apostle speaks not here of theft, or perjury, or murder, or drunkenness, or adultery; but he refers to a total defection or falling away from the Gospel, when a sinner offends not God in some one thing, but entirely renounces his grace."

However we interpret this passage, it is a grave warning—a wake-up call on the sufficiency and finality of Christ.

Illustration from Nature (vv. 7–8)

The reminder that land that produces good crops receives a "blessing of God" (v. 7) illustrates the teaching of this passage. But land that bears nothing but weeds and brush is worthless and "in the end will be burned" (v. 8).

■ *The sin of falling away is the sin of deliber-*
■ *ately, willfully, intentionally rejecting God.*
■ *Hebrews 6:4–8 does not teach that Chris-*
■ *tians can fall from grace, but it does warn*
■ *that if Christian salvation should ever be*
■ *abandoned it could never be recovered.*

CHARACTER OF THE GENUINE BELIEVER (6:9–12)

After his stern warning about falling away from the faith, the author turned immediately to a pastoral expression of affection and encouragement. He focused specifically on those things that pertain to salvation.

Better Things That Accompany Salvation (vv. 9–10)

The writer addresses his readers as "dear friends" (v. 9). They were people to whom the writer was apparently close and for whom he felt special warmth. He expressed confidence in those to whom he wrote. He believed they were bearing fruit as a result of God's salvation in their lives. Fruit gives evidence of righteousness.

Salvation is not simply a theological transaction, a psychological phenomenon, or an emotional experience. Rather it is a reality that translates into Christian character and works of righteousness. Its marks are self-sacrifice, giving, discipline, obedience, and faithfulness. Christians may be assured that their labors are not in vain. Their works and ministries are all known to the Lord.

Paul wrote about the fruit of the Spirit in Galatians 5:22–23: love, joy, peace, patience, kindness, goodness, faithfulness, gentleness, and self-control.

Characteristics of True Believers (vv. 11–12)

"We want each of you to show . . . diligence" (v. 11). Each one is to show spiritual earnestness and confident hope "to the very end."

"We do not want you to become lazy" (v. 12). Christians must avoid sluggishness, realizing that enthusiasm and excitement in the work of the Lord are winsomely contagious.

"Imitate those who through faith and patience inherit what has been promised" (v. 12). The counsel to "imitate" (v. 12) is advice to follow the example of those who worked faithfully and patiently and who always found God absolutely trustworthy.

■ *After his stern warning about falling away*
■ *from the faith, the author focused on the "bet-*
■ *ter things" that accompany salvation and the*
■ *characteristics of true believers.*

SECURITY OF GOD'S PROMISE (6:13–20)

The letter now moves on with a fairly long and involved discussion of God's New Covenant by which believers experience complete security in Christ. When God makes a covenant, He keeps it. His promises are sure. His dealings with Abraham (vv. 13–15) appropriately illustrate "the unchanging nature of his purpose" (v. 17) and show how "it is impossible that God should prove false" (v. 18, NRSV). God's promise was that he would bless Abraham and multiply him (v. 14).

The continuing purpose of God was that "the heirs of the promise" (v. 17, NRSV) maintain absolute confidence in him. The human part of the covenant, however, is not to be ignored, for it must be remembered that it was only when faithful Abraham "patiently endured" that he "obtained the promise" (v. 15, NRSV).

Christians, as latter-day heirs of God's promise to Abraham, the father of the faithful, have taken refuge in Jesus that they may be "greatly encouraged" (v. 18). Believers have a New Covenant and a sure and steadfast anchor in Christ.

Anchor of the Soul

In the ancient world, as ships were entering a harbor, some of the sailors got into a smaller craft and went ahead of the large vessel. Their job was to carry the anchor into the harbor and find a place where it could be securely fastened. In the same way, Jesus went into the inner sanctuary, into the Holy of Holies, the very presence of God, taking with Him the anchor of the soul. *(The Bible Knowledge Commentary: New Testament,* Victor Books, 797.)

■ *When God makes a covenant, He keeps it.*
■ *The writer discussed God's New Covenant by*
■ *which believers experience complete security*
■ *in Christ. He illustrated the unchanging*
■ *nature of God's purpose by recounting God's*
■ *dealings with Abraham.*

QUESTIONS TO GUIDE YOUR STUDY

1. What are the elementary teachings of the faith? What is the writer's point in discussing them?

2. What was the writer teaching in verses 4–6? What was he *not* teaching?

3. What characterizes the true believer?

4. What is the basis of the believer's security in Christ?

In this section of his letter, the author pointed out two features that prove the superiority of the priesthood of Jesus over that of the Aaronic priests. Christ became a high priest by a divine oath which established Him in a new priestly order, the order of Melchizedek.

MELCHIZEDEK THE PRIEST (7:1–10)

As both priest and king, Melchizedek was a type of Christ. The writer mentioned these similarities between the two.

He was a king (vv. 1–2)

The name *Melchizedek* means "king of righteousness" (v. 2). As king of Salem, he was, by translation of the place name *Salem*, the "king of peace" (v. 2).

He was a priest (vv. 1–2)

As "priest of God Most High," he received Abraham's tithes (v. 4) and, symbolically through Abraham, the tithes of all the Levitical priesthood (vv. 5–10).

He had no record of human descendants (v. 3)

As a person "without father or mother, without genealogy," he was without any historical reference regarding his human descendants.

"Like the Son of God he remains a priest forever" (v. 3). Of the eternal Christ, the writer noted that it is not that Jesus resembled Melchizedek but rather that Melchizedek resembled the Son of God. As God's peculiarly ordained priest, Melchizedek both received Abraham's tithes and "blessed him who had the promises" (v. 6). Who is superior and has the power to bless the inferior (v. 7) except one who is especially set apart by "the God Most High"?

■ *As both priest and king, Melchizedek was a*
■ *type of Christ. He was king of Salem. As*
■ *priest of God Most High, he received Abra-*
■ *ham's tithes and, symbolically through Abra-*
■ *ham, the tithes of all the Levitical priesthood.*
■ *The writer of Hebrews declared that he*
■ *resembled the Son of God.*

A HIGH PRIEST LIKE MELCHIZEDEK (7:11–19)

This impressive line of reasoning now moves forward. Perfection was not possible under the Levitical priesthood, so it was necessary for God to raise up the ultimate High Priest, not from the tribe of Levi at all but from the tribe of Judah (vv. 11–14).

"If perfection could have been attained through the Levitical priesthood (for on the basis of it the law was given to the people), why was there still need for another priest to come—one in the order of Melchizedek, not in the order of Aaron?" (v. 11).

Jesus was God's great High Priest not "on the basis of a regulation as to his ancestry but on the basis of the power of an indestructible life" (v. 16). The centuries saw other high priests come and go, receiving their office by inheritance and relinquishing it at death. Jesus, however, knew no such limitation, for as God's Son He has life indestructible and eternal. In Him Christians have life, abundant and everlasting.

The "former regulation" concerning the Levitical priesthood is now set aside "because it was weak and useless" (v. 18). In Jesus Christ, "a better hope is introduced, by which we draw near to

"Perfection"

This word means "perfection, reaching the goal." "It denotes a fulfillment, completion, perfection, an end accomplished as the effect of a process." (*Vine's Complete Expository Dictionary of Old and New Testament Words* [Nashville: Thomas Nelson, 1996,] 467.) The Old Testament Law and the Levitical system could not produce forgiveness or the holiness of heart demanded by God. It failed to provide an adequate relation to God. (Fritz Rienecker, *Linguistic Key to the Greek New Testament* [Grand Rapids: Zondervan, 1980], 686.)

God" (v. 19). No longer do we need a human mediator to approach God on our behalf. By this "better hope" every believer, through Christ, personally draws near to God. Nowhere in the Bible is the profoundly important Christian doctrine of the priesthood of the believer so beautifully stated and so clearly explained as in this passage in Hebrews.

■ *Perfection was not possible under the Leviti-*
■ *cal priesthood, so it was necessary for God to*
■ *raise up the truly ultimate High Priest. No*
■ *longer do we need a human mediator to*
■ *approach God on our behalf. By this "better*
■ *hope" every believer, through Christ, person-*
■ *ally draws near to God.*

JESUS, THE SUPERIOR PRIEST (7:20–28)

God's Guarantee (vv. 20–22)

That Jesus is "the guarantee of a better covenant" (v. 22) means that God's Son is the certain guarantee of God's agreement to save and to bless. The covenant is still God's covenant with faithful people like Abraham.

Of Abraham God said, "For I have chosen him, so that he will direct his children and his household after him to keep the way of the Lord by doing what is right and just" (Gen. 18:19).

A Trustworthy Priest (vv. 23–25)

The generations of earthly priests lived and died. Jesus lives forever, and His priesthood is permanent. He stands ready at all times to save those who come to God through Him. His continuing purpose is to intercede for His people (v. 25).

A Perfect Sin Offering (vv. 26–28)

Jesus is unlike the priests of the Levitical priesthood in the fact that He has made a once-for-all offering for sin (v. 27). What He has done is sufficient to save those who call on Him. Our great High Priest is "holy, blameless, pure, set apart from sinners" (v. 26), a perfect High Priest and a perfect sin offering. This is God's "Son, who has been made perfect forever" (v. 28).

■ *Jesus is God's agreement to save and to bless.*
■ *His priesthood is superior to the Levitical*
■ *priesthood.*

QUESTIONS TO GUIDE YOUR STUDY

1. Why is Melchizedek significant to the writer's argument?
2. How is Christ's priesthood "perfect"?
3. What does the writer mean by declaring that Jesus is the "guarantee of a better covenant"? (v. 22).
4. God is committed to His covenant with us. What is the responsibility on the human side of the agreement?

In this chapter the author of Hebrews indicated that, in addition to beginning a new order of priesthood, Christ inaugurated a New Covenant.

THE NEW ORDER OF PRIESTHOOD (8:1-6)

The writer of Hebrews pointed out that Christians have in Jesus a Mediator who "sat down at the right hand of the throne of the Majesty in heaven, and who serves in the sanctuary, the true tabernacle set up by the Lord, not by man" (vv. 1-2). Priests on earth, offering gifts according to the law, have always worked in a tent made with human hands according to the divine pattern given by God to Moses.

The earthly sanctuary is but "a copy and shadow of what is in heaven" (v. 5). The old covenant was incomplete and therefore flawed. The New Covenant mediated by Jesus, the Son of God Himself, is better because "it is founded on better promises" (v. 6). Likewise, His ministry is superior to the ministry of the priests under the old covenant. Christ's is a ministry of Incarnation, self-denial, suffering, and final self-sacrifice.

Christ is the great Intercessor, praying for His disciples while on earth and continuing to do so in heaven (John 17; Rom. 8:34). He is the supreme High Priest who enters once for all into the sanctuary to make a sacrifice of Himself that brings eternal redemption (Heb. 9:11-12).

Mediator

The term *mediator* in the New Testament bore several ideas. Primarily it meant an umpire or peacemaker who came between two contestants, a negotiator who established a certain relationship, or some neutral person who could guarantee an agreement reached (of Moses in negative sense in Gal. 3:19-28). Christ is the only necessary Mediator (1 Tim. 2:5). Full communion with God comes through faith in the Mediator who gave Himself a ransom for others, mediating a new eternal covenant through His sacrificial death (Heb. 7:22-25; 8:6; 9:15; 12:24).

■ *Christians have in Jesus a Mediator who is*
■ *seated at the right hand of the throne of Maj-*
■ *esty in heaven. Jesus is the great Intercessor,*
■ *praying for His disciples on earth. He is the*
■ *supreme High Priest whose self-sacrifice*
■ *brings eternal redemption.*

THE SUPERIOR COVENANT OF CHRIST (8:7–13)

In addition to beginning a new order of priesthood, Christ inaugurated a New Covenant. It provided three benefits for those who lived under it. The covenant of Christ is superior in these three areas:

1. The New Covenant offered an internalization of the Law.
2. Christ's covenant provided a new, direct knowledge of God.
3. The New Covenant promised complete forgiveness of sins.

Jeremiah 31:31–34 is the longest passage directly quoted in Hebrews. The author calls on one of the major Old Testament prophets to illustrate his point that the old covenant was inadequate, requiring that God mandate a New Covenant. With prophetic vision, Jeremiah had foreseen the day when God would establish a New Covenant with His people (Heb. 8:8), not like the one originally made when He first took them by the hand and led them out of bondage (v. 9). "They did not remain faithful to my covenant, and I turned away from them," God said.

In Jesus, the promised New Covenant with God's people is realized: "I will put my laws into their minds and write them on their hearts. I will be their God, and they will be my people. No longer will a man teach his neighbor, or a man his brother, saying, 'Know the Lord,' because they all know me, from the least of them to the greatest. For I will forgive their wickedness and will remember their sins no more" (vv. 10–12).

The author of Hebrews then commented that Jeremiah's reference to a New Covenant treated the old covenant even then as already essentially obsolete. He concluded this lesson with the observation that "what is obsolete and aging will soon disappear" (v. 13).

■ *Christ's covenant with God's people is supe-*
■ *rior in three ways: (1) it provided a new*
■ *awareness of God's laws and a new nature*
■ *by which to obey God; (2) it gave a personal*
■ *knowledge of God that inspired a loyalty*
■ *and commitment to Him; and (3) it provided*
■ *a complete forgiveness of sins (8:8–12).*
■ *Christians today have inherited the benefits*
■ *of this New Covenant in their relationship*
■ *with God.*

QUESTIONS TO GUIDE YOUR STUDY

1. As our great High Priest, Jesus sacrificed Himself. What did His sacrifice accomplish?
2. What does Christ accomplish as our Mediator?
3. In what ways is Christ's New Covenant superior to the old covenant?
4. The writer declares the old covenant "obsolete." In what ways does Christ's New Covenant render it obsolete?

"Obsolete"

This word means "to declare or treat as old or obsolete." The word was used in the papyri for a temple and a wall which had become old and obsolete and needed repairing. (Fritz Rienecker, *Linguistic Key to the Greek New Testament* [Grand Rapids: Zondervan, 1980,] 692.)

The author shared several effects of Christ's sacrifice to demonstrate its superiority. The death of Christ was more effective than the sacrifices offered by the Aaronic priests because Christ's sacrifice cleansed the conscience, brought forgiveness, and dealt with heavenly realities, not mere earthly symbols.

A SACRIFICE THAT CLEANSES CONSCIENCE (9:1–14)

The First Covenant (vv. 1–10)

The first covenant included regulations for formal worship (v. 1). The author gave a concise but adequate description of the outer tabernacle, called the "Holy Place," and the inner tabernacle, called "the Most Holy Place."

The priests continually went into the outer tabernacle or tent for the performance of their ritual duties (v. 6). The high priest went into the inner tent once a year on the Day of Atonement to make a blood offering for his own sins and for the sins of the people (v. 7). While the outer tabernacle still stood, the way into the Holy of Holies was not disclosed (v. 8).

This inability of the priests to go beyond the Holy Place and into the Holy of Holies was a symbol of that time (v. 9). According to the old arrangement, sacrifices were made for sins, but those sacrifices could not "clear the conscience" of the worshiper (v. 9). Instead they dealt only with regulations imposed "until the time of the new order" (v. 10), washings for the body but not for the heart, gifts for time but not for eternity, sacrifices for sins but not a perfect sacrifice for all sin. In Jesus the time of reformation came, and God's great drama of redemption was perfected.

The Second Covenant (vv. 11–14)

The second covenant was brought into effect by a sacrifice of an entirely different order from the first covenant. Christ entered through an earthly tabernacle—one that is part of creation. He did not bring with him the blood of animals. Christ entered a more perfect tabernacle with his own blood. Christ's blood, offered through the Holy Spirit, brought about a radical change in the hearts of those who received His gift. This change cleanses the consciences of works that lead to death. The believer is prepared to serve the living God.

The author of Hebrews combined the concept of the high priest with that of the blood offering to explain how Jesus both did the high priestly work and made Himself the offering. Jesus did not walk away from suffering. He walked through suffering and death to break sin's dominion over all who want salvation's glorious freedom. This brief passage (vv. 11–14) contains the doctrinal heart of the letter to the Hebrews.

The Holy Places

Holy Place. The courts, the inner room, and the outer room of the tabernacle (Exod. 26:33). Later the expression was used in reference to the Temple and its environs. It was a holy place in the sense of being a place set apart for Yahweh.

Holy of Holies. This was the innermost sanctuary of the tabernacle and later the Temple. It was separated from the other parts of the Temple by a thick curtain. The holy of holies was specially associated with the presence of Yahweh. In the early years of the existence of the Temple, the holy of holies contained the ark of the covenant.

In the light of the great truth that Christians are cleansed by the blood of Christ to serve God, it is important to consider the service God expects. The matter will surface later in the letter, but at this point we should observe that the intention of "service" here is not formal worship. The recurring emphasis on obedience, growth, maturity, and the things that accompany salvation argue for assigning a meaning to *service* which would encompass the doing of truth, righteousness, justice, and peace. When questioned about what reasonable service to God might have as its absolute minimum, Jesus answered that we are to love God with our entire being and our neighbors as ourselves (Matt. 22:34–40).

■ *The old covenant made provision for remov-*
■ *ing external pollution by the use of animal*
■ *sacrifices and familiar rituals. Under the*
■ *New Covenant Jesus surrendered His life to*
■ *God in sacrifice for sin. The sacrifice of*
■ *Christ is more effective for us today in three*
■ *ways. First, it did not limit itself to the mere*
■ *removal of ceremonial pollution. It cleansed*
■ *the conscience from guilt and thus inspired*
■ *holy living.*

A SACRIFICE THAT REMOVES SIN (9:15–22)

The death of Christ redeems believers from the sins that would have left them dead under the old covenant (v. 15). In dying, Jesus became the "mediator of the new covenant, that those who are called may receive the promised inheritance" (v. 15). The author continued this careful line of reasoning. Where a will is involved, the death of the one who made it must be verified (v. 16). A will takes effect only at the death of the one making it (v. 17). The first covenant was not ratified except by the life blood that signified life given (v.18).

Then, "when every commandment of the Law had been declared by Moses" (RSV), he took the blood of the sacrificial animals and sprinkled the book of the law, the people, the tent, and the vessels used in the formal ceremony of worship (vv. 19–21). Moses' words, "This is the blood of the covenant, which God commanded you to keep" (v. 20), remind readers of Hebrews that "under the law almost everything is purified with blood, and without the shedding of blood there is no forgiveness of sins" (v. 22, NRSV).

This profound theological insight is not one believers today may ignore. This is the heart of the gospel. Preaching or teaching that ignores this isn't the gospel of Jesus Christ.

- Christ's sacrifice resulted in the removal of
- sin by the shedding of Christ's blood.

A SACRIFICE THAT AFFECTS HEAVENLY REALITIES (9:23–28)

The writer continued a vivid comparison between animal sacrifices under the old covenant with Jesus' sacrifice. Under the old covenant it was necessary for both the tabernacle and the things in it to be purified through prescribed rites (v. 21). "The heavenly things" (v. 23), the things of heaven itself, are somehow purified and given special glory and honor in the presence of the crucified and risen and ascended Lamb of God whose "better" sacrifice transforms not only earth but also heaven itself. He entered not into an earthly tent of sanctuary but "into heaven itself, now to appear in the presence of God on our behalf" (vv. 23–24). Christ does not offer Himself repeatedly but "once for all at the end of the age to put away sin by the sacrifice of himself" (v. 26, RSV).

The Greek word translated "judgment" (v. 27) when transliterated into English letters, makes our word *crisis*. The crisis of final determination of the everlasting fate of every person will come after death at the time of judgment.

In the normal course of human events people die, and they are not then allowed to come back to life in this world to start all over again (v. 27). As judgment follows death in the normal course

"Blood"

Hebrews 9 has twelve references to *blood*, more than in any other entire book of the New Testament with the exception of Revelation, which also has twelve references to blood. This emphasis on blood represents a major concern for the life of the people of God by the sacrifice of the life of God's Son.

The term *blood of Christ* in the New Testament designates the atoning death of Christ. *Atonement* refers to the basis and process by which estranged people become at one with God. At His last Passover, Jesus inaugurated the New Covenant in His blood "shed for many for the remission of sins" (Matt. 26:28; cp. Luke 22:20, NKJV). Jesus died as a sin-bearer that we might live for righteousness and become healed (1 Pet. 2:24).

of human events, so Christ's sinless life and sacrificial death will not be repeated. However, "he will appear a second time, not to bear sin" as He did on the Cross, "but to bring salvation to those who are waiting for him" (v. 28).

Christians are not to fear the judgment of the Lord. Instead, we joyfully anticipate the Second Coming when there will be a final consummation in eternity of our salvation that began in time.

- *By entering God's presence, Christ showed*
- *that He has offered a perfect sacrifice.*
- *Because Christ has fully removed all sins,*
- *Christians have the hope that He will one day*
- *return to complete their salvation by taking*
- *them to be with the Father.*

QUESTIONS TO GUIDE YOUR STUDY

1. What is the first covenant? the second covenant?
2. What acts lead to death?
3. What does the blood of Christ do in the believer's heart?
4. What should be the believer's response to being cleansed by the blood of Christ?

In the first part of this chapter the author explained the permanence of Christ's sacrifice. Because His once-for-all death forever took away all sins, there remains no further need for sacrifice.

In the second half, the writer explained that because Christians now have complete access to God, they can draw near to Him with an inward and outward cleansing. He expressed several concerns along these lines. Finally, as a body of believers, Christians need to consider how to stimulate one another to good works by meeting together.

CHRIST'S PERMANENT SACRIFICE (10:1–18)

The Law Is "Only a Shadow" (vv. 1–9)

The writer is about to bring to a close his exhaustive statement about Abraham, Moses, Melchizedek, the tabernacle, the Levitical priesthood, the high priests, and the sin offerings. The Law and the sacrifices are but shadows of the true redemption achieved through Christ's sacrifice.

These acts of sacrifice did not bring to perfection those for whom they were offered year after year. The writer asked a rhetorical question. Would these sacrifices have ceased if they had cleansed the people? He followed this question with an assertion: It's impossible for the blood of bulls and goats to take away sin. Only Christ through His perfect obedience to death can accomplish the removal of sin and the perfection of sinners.

"Shadow"

This word refers to the outline or shadow cast by the object, which is the reality. In the New Testament, it is used of ceremonies under the law and its sacrifices and offerings (Col. 2:17).

The writer quoted from a psalm of David, Psalm 40:6–8:

"Therefore, when Christ came into the world, he said: 'Sacrifice and offering you did not desire, but a body you prepared for me; with burnt offerings and sin offerings you were not pleased. Then I said, 'Here I am—it is written about me in the scroll—I have come to do your will, O God'" (Heb. 10:5-7).

Christ's Sacrifice Is Superior (vv. 10–18)

Once-for-All. The death of Christ was more effective than the sacrifices offered by the Aaronic priests because Christ's sacrifice cleansed the conscience, brought forgiveness, and dealt with heavenly realities, not mere earthly symbols. Christ's sacrifice was also superior because He offered Himself voluntarily in a once-for-all, never-to-be-repeated death.

The author then quoted from Jeremiah 31:33: "'This is the covenant I will make with them after that time, says the Lord. I will put my laws in their hearts, and I will write them on their minds.' Then he adds: 'Their sins and lawless acts I will remember no more'" (Heb. 10:16–17).

All Christians are sanctified. Having come to earth to do the Father's will, He abolished the old order and established a new order (v. 10). According to the will of God, "we have been holy through the sacrifice of the body of Jesus Christ once for all" (v. 10). All Christians are sanctified by Christ who brings us pure, spotlessly cleansed by His own blood, before the Father.

We have no further need for sacrifice. When Christ's great high priestly work was finished, "he sat down at the right hand of God. Since that time he waits for his enemies to be made his footstool" (vv. 12–13). By His single offering of Himself, He "made perfect forever those who are being made holy" (v. 14).

Where such forgiveness is fully given by God in Christ and fully received through personal repentance for sin and personal faith in the Lord Jesus, there need be "no longer any offering for sin" (v. 18, NRSV).

The author of Hebrews carefully shared his mind and heart about these immensely important matters. No more about them needed to be said. The writer of Hebrews finished preaching his sermon; he turned next to the exhortation.

- *The once-for-all death of Christ forever took*
- *away all sins. When these sins are removed,*
- *no further need for sacrifice remains.*

Note: Here the writer of Hebrews began his section on advice for practical Christian living. This part covers the remainder of the letter up to the conclusion (10:19–13:19).

STAMINA IN OBEDIENCE (10:19–39)

Counsel to Draw Near to God and Encourage One Another (vv. 19–25)

By God's grace, Christians can boldly approach Him. Christians are endowed with "confidence to enter the Most Holy Place by the blood of Jesus" (v. 19). They are enabled to live a new life, to walk in "a new and living way" (v. 20). Since we have in Christ "a great priest" (v. 21), we are called to draw near with a true heart "in full assurance of faith" (v. 22). The concept of drawing near to God is a prominent one in this letter, and its use again in this context is particularly important. Needy believers draw near to him for cleansing, for renewal, for strength, for comfort, for help, and for guidance.

The writer urged believers, himself included, to "draw near to God with a sincere heart" (v. 22).

Faith (v. 22). In drawing near to God, the believer's first concern is faith. As Christians draw near to God with a true heart, we are to do so "in full assurance of faith" (v. 22). A primary aim of the writer of Hebrews was to bring his readers to this full assurance of faith, to complete confidence in God, to positive certainty about Him to whom we have committed

"Sincere"

The word translated *sincere* conveys the idea of truth, loyalty, and dependability.

Drawing Near to God

Concern	Verse(s)	Action Involved
Faith	22	Living with complete confidence in God.
Hope	22–23	Enduring trials, conquering temptations, and following righteousness.
Christian Love	24	Acts of kindness and righteousness toward others in Christ's name for His glory.
Good Works	24	To do good without ceasing. Faith, hope, and love all find both validation and fruition in good works.

everything for time and eternity. We must know whom we have believed (2 Tim. 1:12) in order to have this full assurance of faith.

Hope (vv. 22–23). The writer's second concern is hope. He urges his readers, "Let us hold unswervingly to the hope we profess" (v. 23). In hope Christians endure trials, conquer temptations, bear witness, follow righteousness, do the things that make for peace, and await the return of their Lord.

Love (v. 24). The writer's third concern in drawing near to God was love. "Let us consider how we may spur one another on toward love and good deeds" (v. 24). Love is not something we think, say, or feel. Love is something we do. As important as it is, love cannot be taken for granted. It must be stirred up, aroused, fanned into flame, and encouraged.

"Good deeds" (v. 24). A fourth concern in drawing near to God is "good deeds" (v. 24). The writer treated the subject of good deeds in the context of love. Christian love and good works belong together; in fact, they are inseparable.

The writer closed this section with an admonition not to "give up meeting together" (v. 25).

■ *Because Christians have complete access to*
■ *God, they can draw near to Him with an*
■ *inward and outward cleansing. They also*
■ *need to consider how to encourage one*
■ *another to good works by meeting together.*

Warning of Judgment to Fall on the Disobedient (vv. 26–39)

Avoid acts of disobedience. Because Christians "see the Day approaching" (v. 25), the writer of Hebrews listed several acts of disobedience he wanted his readers to avoid:

- They must be vigilant to avoid deliberate sin (v. 26).
- They must also be careful not to spurn the Son of God (v. 29).
- They must not profane the blood of the covenant (v. 29).
- They must not throw away their confidence (v. 35) or shrink back from our commitment (v. 39).

Avoid apostasy. He now returned to the topic he previously dealt with in 6:4–8: apostasy. Perhaps an evil spirit of apostasy was actually working among the particular Christians to whom this letter was originally sent. Or perhaps here, as earlier, he meant to sound the note of grave warning that would keep them decisively turned away from lukewarmness, coldness, and subsequent apostasy.

The deliberate sin in 10:26 is willful, intentional abandonment of Christ after receiving "the knowledge of the truth" (v. 26). If such a thing

The vengeance and judgment of God (v. 30) were in mind when the writer issued this solemn warning: "It is a dreadful thing to fall into the hands of the living God" (v. 31). It was this theme that inspired the preaching of Jonathan Edwards as he called multitudes to repentance in the First Great Awakening in America. Today, we would do well to respond to this warning by cultivating a continuing spirit of personal repentance and personal faith. God's promises of judgment are as certain as His promises of grace, and believers ought never to forget it.

should be, then "no sacrifice for sins is left" (v. 26). Instead there would be "a fearful expectation of judgment and of raging fire that will consume the enemies of God" (v. 27).

Under the Mosaic Law, the death penalty had been prescribed for the twenty-five offenses when guilt was confirmed by "the testimony of two or three witnesses" (v. 28). Such a death was awful; but "how much more severely" will a person be punished who spurns the Son of God and profanes the blood of the covenant by which he was sanctified? (v. 29).

The writer reminded the original recipients of this letter of their struggles and sufferings in the time of persecution through which they had passed. They had been able to endure because they knew they "had better and lasting possessions" (v. 34). He urged them not to "throw away your confidence; it will be richly rewarded" (v. 35).

Persevere in the will of God. Believers are to "persevere," endure to do the will of God and receive what is promised (v. 36). The author then quoted the well-known Habakkuk 2:3–4 to call attention to the fact that the just, or righteous, shall live by faith, but that God can have no pleasure in anyone who shrinks back (vv. 37–38). Christians, however, "are not of those who shrink back and are destroyed, but of those who believe and are saved" (v. 39).

■ *The author warned his readers that turning*
■ *away from Christ would expose them to*
■ *divine judgment. He insisted that his readers*
■ *show genuine faith by their continued com-*
■ *mitment to Christ. They had already suffered*
■ *for their faith, but they needed to demon-*
■ *strate stamina by obeying God.*

QUESTIONS TO GUIDE YOUR STUDY

1. Although the sacrifices of the Levitical system met the needs of the law, why was God not pleased with these sacrifices?
2. What reasons did the writer give to show the superiority of Christ's sacrifice over those of the Levitical priesthood?
3. What specifically did the author warn his readers in about verses 26–39?
4. How does a believer preserve in the will of God?

"Assurance"

The word translated "assurance" by the NRSV is a compound made up of the preposition "under" and the verb "to stand." Literally, it means "a standing under, support." The word has several connotations and usages, such as *essence, substance, foundation, confident assurance,* and *attestation,* that is, documents that attest or provide evidence of ownership. According to Greek scholar A. T. Robertson, this word "is a very common word from Aristotle" and refers to "what stands under anything (a building, a contract, a promise). . . . It is common in the papyri in business documents as the basis or guarantee of transactions." (A. T. Robertson, *Word Pictures in the New Testament,* "The Epistle to the Hebrews," vol.5, 418.)

Hebrews 11 is not only the best-known chapter in this letter, but it is also one of the best-loved chapters in the Bible. It is more than simply a chapter about faith; it is a chapter about *faith in action.* It is about faith at work, faith that does not shrink from battle, faith that does not flee from confrontation, faith that does not bend under pressure, faith that does not wither under the heat of persecution. With almost incomparable beauty and excellence, the author painted a masterpiece of the word picture of faith.

In verses 1–3 the author described the nature of faith as a conviction of certainty about what we do not see. This kind of faith motivated the godly men and women of the past to move toward the promises, even though they did not inherit them (vv. 4–40).

THE NATURE OF FAITH (11:1–3)

What is faith? Verse 1 describes the nature of faith. Notice how these three Bible versions translate this text:

- "Now faith is the substance of things hoped for, the evidence of things not seen" (KJV).
- "Now faith is being sure of what we hope for and certain of what we do not see" (NIV).
- "Now faith is the assurance of things hoped for, the conviction of things not seen" (NRSV).

Faith Is the Foundation for Hope (v. 1)

Faith is the foundation of hope, standing under hope, providing the ground on which hope is built.

Faith Is the Proof of What We Do Not See (v. 1)

What does faith do? It is the evidence, proof, or conviction that enables us to perceive unseen things just as if they were seen, to sense spiritual realities just as truly as we sense things by seeing and smelling, hearing and touching. Faith claims the future in the present. It gives things that are yet to come all the certainty of things that already are. Through faith, unseen things take on substance, and future things take on present reality.

Faith transcends the time-space framework in which we live this present life. It reaches to the high places where eternity can be seen beyond all present boundaries and barriers. By faith we hold clear title to the property of salvation. With faith in our possession, history becomes filled with meanings, life's present puzzle is no longer an insoluble mystery; and the unseen future comes into plain view and into clear focus.

Faith is not the gift of seeing something that is not there. Rather, it is the gift of seeing through all the haze of doubt and the pollution of sin to the distant city of God set on the mountain of eternity. Faith is not believing something in spite of the evidence; it is living life for the Lord God in scorn of all earthly consequences.

Faith Receives God's Approval (v. 2)

By faith, our spiritual forebears "were commended" (v. 2). As they demonstrated their trust in God, He affirmed and blessed them.

Faith in God's Creative Word (v. 3)

"By faith we understand that the worlds were prepared by the word of God" (v. 3, NRSV). Scientists continually come forward with new theories about the when of Creation. The how

"Evidence"

The words *evidence* or *conviction* carries the concept of proof. The word was used in the papyri for legal proofs of an accusation. The word *conviction* implies an outward response of the inner assurance of faith. "When the Holy Spirit gives us faith through the Word, the very presence of that faith in our hearts is all the assurance and evidence we need!" (Warren W. Wiersbe, *Wiersbe's Expository Outlines on the New Testament* [Wheaton, Ill.: Victor Books], 706.)

"Faith is like a muscle. As we exercise it, it grows and develops. God asks us to do that today. He does not want us to take His Word for granted. He wants us to check it out. He wants us to commit ourselves to Him and see if He will not do what He has promised. Faith is the substance, the title deed of the things we hope for and desire. Everthing we dream for in life is ours by faith."—James T. Draper of Creation, however, is a theological perception to which the author of Hebrews spoke with profound insight. By faith we understand that, whenever it was done, Creation was done "by the word of God" that He made the material out of the immaterial, "that what is seen was made out of things which do not appear" (v. 3, RSV).

The writer's point here is that his readers believed that God created the universe even though they did not witness it. They accepted the fact of Creation through the power of His word by faith, not sight. In a sense, they had a start in faith.

John Calvin said this verse teaches the same truth as Romans 1:20, "where it is said, that the invisible things of God are made known to us by the creation of the world, they being seen in his works. God has given us, throughout the whole framework of this world, clear evidences of his eternal wisdom, goodness, and power; and though he is in himself invisible, he in a manner becomes visible to us in his works" (*Commentary on Hebrews*).

- *Faith is the support for the believer's hope.*
- *It gives reality to things that cannot be seen.*
- *It is evidence that God is absolutely trustworthy and that His promises are completely sure. By this faith Old Testament believers received a positive witness from God.*

FAITH IN ACTION: THE ROLL CALL (11:4–40)

This chapter often has been called the Westminster Abbey of the Old Testament, for as the great London cathedral contains the graves and appropriate markers for most of the famous men and women of the British Empire, so this passage contains appropriate markers for many of the great men and women who are the spiritual giants of the Bible.

The writer's purpose for the illustrations that follow is to show how faith was put into action by men and women like ourselves. These illustrations are windows. Like the parables of Jesus, when appropriately used, they provide earthly examples with heavenly meanings. It is heavenly meaning, not the details of history, with which the writer was primarily concerned.

Abel: Worshiping in Faith (v. 4)
By faith Abel offered a better sacrifice than Cain. Abel received God's approval as righteous but not because he used the right words. Instead, it was his right deed, his offering to God of the better or more acceptable sacrifice, that God approved. Although Abel died, his faith still speaks to us today about the importance of obedient and active faith.

Enoch: Walking in Faith (vv. 5–6)
We know from the Old Testament that Enoch "walked with God" (Gen. 5:24) by faith and that he "was taken from this life, so that he did not experience death" (v. 5). Enoch's communion with God was so complete that his journey from time to eternity was not interrupted by the detour of death. In active faith, Enoch walked with the Lord and by so doing "pleased God" (v. 5).

Whoever comes to God in faith for salvation must use the mind so as to understand both God's existence and His justice in rewarding those who seek His face. Faith expects great things from God and attempts great things for Him.

Noah: Obeying by Faith (v. 7)
Noah is the first specific example of faith given. God warned Noah that a Flood was coming. He commanded Noah to build an ark that would save him and his family in the coming deluge. After being warned by God of the Flood to come, by faith Noah constructed an ark to save his household (v. 7). Noah had no evidence of

"Translated"

The Greek word used here is "one of the most beautiful words to be found in the Bible." It means "to replace." "We could put it like this, 'Enoch was transposed.' He exchanged earth for heaven. God loved him so much, and he was so true to God, that God just took him on to glory." (James T. Draper, *Hebrews*, 307.)

Faith pleases God. In fact, without faith, pleasing God is impossible. Faith is manifest in two ways: (1) The person believes that God exists and (2) that God rewards those who seek Him. The demons believe that God exists (James 2:19), but they do not respond to His righteous character, which demands that they cease to do evil and learn to do well (Isa. 1:16–18).

what was about to happen except what God told him. He believed God and built the ark.

Abraham: The Life of Faith (vv. 8–12, 17–19)

Abraham, the father of the faithful, holds the place of greatest prominence in this list. The Genesis account tells us that Abraham believed God and that God reckoned it to him as righteousness (Gen. 15:6). This passage in Hebrews highlights his life of faith.

- In response to God's call, Abraham obeyed and left his ancestral home. He didn't have anything like a complete picture of where he was going or the outcome of his journey, but he believed God and obeyed (v. 8).

- Abraham lived or sojourned as a stranger, in the land God would later give his descendents. He lived in tents as did his son, Isaac, and his grandson, Jacob. He was content with these arrangements because he was looking for a substantial city—one God had built (v. 10).

- Abraham exhibited exceptional faith when he responded to God's command to sacrific Isaac. He recognized God's ownership of Isaac and believed that God could raise Isaac from death (v. 19).

Sarah: The Power of Faith (v. 11)

Because she is a heroine of the faith, Sarah received special attention. By faith Sarah received power to conceive, even when she was past the age of childbearing. Conception, birth, and child rearing require concentration of strength, energy, and will. Sarah's faith was so active that it reckoned God "faithful who had made the promise" (v. 11) to enable her, even in old age, to receive such blessing.

"Sojourned"

"This verb is related to a noun which refers to a licensed sojourner. Such a person paid for the privilege of living in a land without becoming a citizen in order to do business in the land." (Herschel H. Hobbs, *Hebrews*, 113.)

Because the writer of the letter did not want his readers to forget his main point with these illustrations, he paused a moment to remind them of his purpose before continuing (vv. 13–16). All of these—Abel, Enoch, Noah, Abraham, and Sarah—"died in faith" without receiving the complete realization of the promises of God. With eyes of faith, they saw "from a distance" the promise of God's redemption and greeted it, remaining essentially "strangers . . . on the earth" (v. 13, NRSV).

This review reminds us also not to set our own minds to things on earth. We, too, are sojourners on our way to a better country. We are to maintain an orientation to God's unfolding future.

The writer proceeded to mention briefly several other Old Testament heroes and heroines of the faith.

Others (vv. 20–40)

Isaac. Like his father Abraham, Isaac believed God and acted on his faith by passing on his blessing to Jacob and Esau and, through that blessing, to succeeding generations. (v. 20). He showed faith that his own death would not cancel out the promises of God.

Jacob. Likewise Jacob, "when he was dying, blessed each of Joseph's sons" (v. 21) as a sign that he was looking ahead to the future for the fulfillment of the promises of God. Although famine had forced Jacob and his family to emigrate to Egypt, his ties to the land of promise were not severed, and his confidence in the promises of God was not shaken.

Joseph. By faith Joseph is said to have spoken at the end of his life of "the exodus of the Israelites" and to have given them instructions to take his bones back for burial in the Land of Promise, when they themselves returned (v. 22).

Moses. By faith Moses' parents hid him to save his life (v. 23). By faith Moses identified with the

Israelites, refusing to be called the son of Pharaoh's daughter. He chose to suffer with God's people rather than indulge in the pleasures of sin (v. 25).

Rahab. By faith, the life of Rahab the harlot was spared. She did not perish with the disobedient "because she welcomed the spies" (v. 31), thus proving herself to be believing.

As the writer of Hebrews drew to the end of his roll call, he also mentioned Gideon, Barak, Samson, Jephthah, David, Samuel, and the prophets (vv. 33–34).

This great chapter concludes with this summary: "These were all commended for their faith, yet none of them received what had been promised. God had planned something better for us so that only together with us would they be made perfect" (vv. 39–40).

These people lived in faith, worked in faith, and died in faith. God was the object of their faith. He did great things for them under the old covenant promise, and He has done and is doing something far better for us under the New Covenant through Christ.

■ *As an incentive to his readers' endurance*
■ *before God, the writer presented a gallery of*
■ *Old Testament heroes of faith. We, too, are*
■ *sojourners on our way to a better country.*
■ *We are to maintain an orientation to God's*
■ *unfolding future. By faith, like those in the*
■ *writer's roll call, we too, are to cling to righ-*
■ *teousness and unchanging values.*

QUESTIONS TO GUIDE YOUR STUDY

1. According to the writer of Hebrews, what is faith?
2. What does faith do?
3. What are we to learn from the author's list of Old Testament illustrations of faith? Why is each example included?
4. Because Rahab was a harlot, some people might be reluctant to include her in a hall of fame of faith. Why did the writer of Hebrews include her here?

In this chapter the writer of Hebrews provided incentives to the believer for enduring hardships. He mentioned the example of Jesus (vv. 1–3) and the benevolent discipline of God (vv. 4–11). Describing the dramatic circumstances under which the old covenant began, he presented Jesus as the Mediator of a New and better Covenant (vv. 18–29).

To promote holiness and fear in the readers, the writer noted that the character of God resembles a consuming fire.

"Cloud"

We find the word *cloud* used only here in the New Testament. It is the Greek word for a vast mass of clouds (*nephos*). The metaphor refers to the great amphitheater with the arena for the runners and the tiers upon tiers of seats rising like a cloud. The "witnesses" here are not mere spectators but those who testify from their own experience to God's fulfilling His promises (11:2, 4, 5, 33, 39). (A. T. Robertson, *Word Pictures in the New Testament*, "The Epistle to the Hebrews," vol. 5, 432.)

AN ADMONITION TO PUT FAITH TO WORK (12:1–13)

The Example of Christ (vv. 1–3)

The author of Hebrews wrote that we are surrounded by "a great cloud of witnesses" (v. 1).

Because Christians are surrounded by a great "cloud of witnesses," they are called to action (v 1). They are to "throw off everything that hinders" so that their working faith will not be frustrated. Our God-given freedom guarantees that we may choose to run with handicaps, that we may pet the sin that dogs our feet, but we will do well to lay aside every hindering weight and shun every distraction and sin.

The purpose of this personal initiative to reject sin is that Christians may "run with perseverance" (v. 1) the race marked out for them. The example of Christ should motivate and encourage the believer so that he or she "will not grow weary and lose heart" (v. 3).

- Believers are to lay aside every hindering
- weight and shun every distracting and hob-
- bling sin so they may "run with persever-
- ance" the race marked out for them. They
- are to look to the example of Christ as an
- encouragement.

God's Purpose (vv. 4–13)

Christians are to demonstrate subjection to God by their obedience in suffering and through trials, by patient endurance of hostility, and even through open persecution (v. 9). The result of this endurance is "a harvest of righteousness and peace for those who have been trained by it" (v. 11). The writer of Hebrews issued three exhortations to his readers as a track for discipline:

1. *"Strengthen your feeble arms"* (v. 12). The writer's reference to weak hands and feeble knees is from Isaiah 35:3, where the prophet was encouraging the people to endure with the assurance that God would come and save them.

2. Strengthen your *"weak knees"* (v. 12). Believers need strength for the heavy loads they will lift and the hard tasks they will undertake.

3. *"Make level paths for your feet"* (v. 13). The path is to be level so that the "lame may not be disabled, bur rather healed." Runners leave tracks behind them that either lead or mislead others who follow. The path of the believer is not to be "turned out of the way" (A. T. Robertson, *Word Pictures in the New Testament*, "The Epistle to the Hebrews," vol.5, 437).

"Throw off"

"Throw off" is a compound word made up of the preposition *off* and the verb *to throw.* A. T. Robertson wrote that "the runners ran in the stadium nearly naked." For the believer, *everything* is "every encumbrance that handicaps like doubt, pride, sloth, anything. No trailing garment to hinder or trip one." (*Word Pictures in the New Testament*, "The Epistle to the Hebrews," vol.5, 432).

It is God's intention that Christians should march into spiritual battle in full spiritual health and vibrant faith. The door to God was opened through Jesus Christ, and we are to walk confidently through that door and in His way.

- *The writer also found encouragement for*
- *endurance from Jesus' example (12:1–11).*
- *Jesus had already run the race of faith, and*
- *God had placed Him on the throne. When*
- *Christians consider the hardships He faced,*
- *they can find strength and fresh courage.*
- *God allows all Christians to experience*
- *hardship so that they might develop holiness.*
- *Even though God's chastisement seems hard*
- *for the time, it will eventually produce righ-*
- *teousness in those who follow Him.*

A WARNING AGAINST REJECTING GOD (12:14–29)

The Beauty of Holiness (vv. 14–17)

A Call for Holiness (v. 14). Hebrews 12:14 is one of the great ethical texts in the Bible. It is a clarion call for holiness. After reminding his readers of how discipline from the Lord comes so "that we may share in his holiness" (v. 10). They are "to live in peace with all men."

The "peace with all men" for which we are to strive is a natural result of one's peace with God. Such peace, however, is not a routine result. The believer must determine to work out a right relationship with God and right relationships with others. The believer achieves true peace with others by working faithfully for the things that make for peace: justice and righteousness,

"We may wonder why God wants us to follow after peace before holiness, as our text suggests. We need to remind ourselves that Christians are being reminded that they cannot be right with God if they are not right with their fellowmen. A lost man must get right with God first, and then with his fellowman. But a Christian cannot be right with God if he is not right with his fellowman." (James T. Draper, *Hebrews*, 347.)

honesty and fairness, selflessness and kindness, mercy and love.

Holiness Is Available to Those in Christ (v. 14). Holiness is available to those who come to Christ in faith and then strive for it with all their hearts. It is sobering to realize that without holiness, "no one will see the Lord" (v. 14).

The Root of Bitterness (vv. 15–16). The author next issued a three-dimensioned admonition. Believers are to "see to it":

1. "That no one fail to obtain the grace of God."
2. "That no root of bitterness springs up and causes trouble, and through it the many become defiled."
3. That no one be immoral or irreligious like Esau, "who sold his birthright for a single meal" (NRSV).

The "root of bitterness" is a reference from Deuteronomy 29:18 that warns against turning away from the Lord. As tares could choke out the wheat in Bible times, and as Johnson grass can ruin a crop in our times, so the Christian is to ensure that no bitter root of evil doctrine or evil doing is allowed to grow in the garden of faith, lest trouble and defilement prevail.

Sexual Immorality and Godlessness (vv. 15–16). Christians also are to "see to it . . . that no one is sexually immoral, or is godless." The first reference seems to be to sexual immorality. The word used is the one from which our word *pornography* is derived. The word is generally taken to mean sexual vice and is most frequently translated "fornication." The second warning against being irreligious or profane is bolstered by a stern reminder of the awful fate of Esau who so despised the heritage which should have

Holiness is a drawing near to God with a cleansed conscience. The Bible provides several reasons we as believers need holiness:

1. We need holiness because God commands it: "Be holy; because I am holy" (Lev. 20:7; 1 Peter 1:16).
2. We need holiness because our nature is such that we can never be at rest until we are at rest in God who is holy.
3. We need holiness because holiness in the lives of believers is the only thing to which the lost world has ever paid attention. It is the only thing in the world that authenticates our faith to the lost multitudes.

"See to it"

The writer of Hebrews used this phrase repeatedly throughout this passage. It is one word in the Greek text. It is made up of the words *over* and *to watch*. It means "to watch over, to watch out for." This verb is a present-tense participle, indicating that this action is to be continuous. "The word expresses that careful regard of those who occupy a position of responsibility (as a physician, or a superintendent)." (Fritz Rienecker, *Linguistic Key to the Greek New Testament* [Grand Rapids: Zondervan, 1980], 716.)

been his in line with the promises of God that he sold it all "for a single meal" (v. 16). Christians are to be everlastingly vigilant to "see to it" that none be sexually immoral or profanely irreligious. Those qualities are outward signs of inner chaos.

■ *God provides the Christian with another*
■ *incentive for endurance. God desires that all*
■ *persons seek after holiness.*

Requirement for Grateful Service (vv. 18–29)

Christians have not come to Mount Sinai with its terrifying manifestations of the awful presence of the Almighty (vv. 18–21) but "to Mount Zion and to the city of the living God, the heavenly Jerusalem" (NRSV). If the former was awesome, how much more awesome is the city of God.

God shook the earth at Sinai. Many who saw the display of power and holiness at Sinai still refused to listen and obey. As a result, they died in the desert, outside the land God had promised them.

God is going to shake the earth again and not only the earth but heaven as well. The result of this shaking will be that only those things which are unshakable will remain. Everything else will be consumed.

Christians are called to be grateful for "receiving a kingdom that cannot be shaken" (v. 28). As a consequence, and never forgetting that "our God is a consuming fire" (v. 29), we are to "worship God acceptably with reverence and awe" (v. 28).

■ God will not tolerate a disobedient,
■ self-serving lifestyle. The presence of God at
■ Sinai caused thunder, lightning, and fright
■ among the people who saw Him. If God's
■ speaking on earth at Sinai produced fear,
■ how much more would His words from
■ heaven through Jesus produce fear. God's
■ kingdom is unmovable. This gives Chris-
■ tians the grace to serve Him with stamina
■ and reverence.

QUESTIONS TO GUIDE YOUR STUDY

1. The author of Hebrews wrote that Christians are surrounded by "a great cloud of
witnesses." What does this phrase mean?
2. What is the content of the author's warning against rejecting God?
3. What is the main point of the author's
relating Old Testament experiences in
verses 18–29?
4. What is the relationship between a Christian's salvation and grateful service?

"Many years ago President Pat Neff of Baylor University commented on laying up treasures in heaven. He said that preachers had been telling him to do this, but that no one had told him how to get his treasures into heaven. He concluded that to do this one must invest his earthly treasure in things that are going to heaven. Not cattle, land, stocks, bonds, oil, or other earthy things—but in men, women, boys, and girls." (Hershel H. Hobbs, *Hebrews*, 131.)

This chapter contains the writer's final exhortations and conclusion. The letter of Hebrews is profoundly theological, and its emphasis on the great high priestly work of Christ is unsurpassed in the Bible. It is deeply ethical, however, from its beginning to its ending. In the last chapter of the book, ethical issues of great importance are raised and dealt with by the writer in the knowledge that Christians need help in knowing how to live while seeking the city of God. The writer did not conclude his letter with chapter 12. Instead, he climaxed it with chapter 13 and its immensely important moral teachings.

EXHORTATIONS FOR CHRISTIAN BEHAVIOR TOWARD OTHERS (13:1–3)

The writer delivered these exhortations regarding the believer's behavior toward others.

"Keep on loving each other as brothers" (v. 1)

Where the Spirit of Christ is, there is brotherly love. Christians are not to let their brotherly love fade. Instead, they are to cultivate it diligently.

"Do not forget to entertain strangers" (v. 2)

This exhortation shows the importance of hospitality as an expression of brotherly love among the early Christians. By showing such hospitality, many have entertained "angels," the messengers of God, "without knowing it." Some risks are taken when strangers are entertained, but living the Christian life was never meant to be a risk-free adventure. The moral ministry of hospitality, therefore, is not to be neglected.

"Remember those in prison . . . and those who are mistreated" (v. 3)

This exhortation reminds us that Christians are to maintain a deeply genuine concern for common, poor, powerless, and downtrodden people of the world. The writer was not claiming the innocence of most prisoners but rather that they are all needy, lonely, and frustrated by their self-made shackles inside their society-made walls. We are to remember them as if we were there with them, in the knowledge that, as we render moral ministries to them and to needy people like them in Jesus' name, we actually serve our Lord (Matt. 25:31–46).

When John Calvin wrote his commentary on Hebrews in the sixteenth century, he observed that hospitality had, at that time, ceased to be practiced by most people. "For the ancient hospitality, celebrated in histories, is unknown to us, and inns now supply the place of accommodations for strangers."

■ *Christians have practical duties with one*
■ *another. They must show sympathy to oth-*
■ *ers, including those in prison.*

EXHORTATIONS FOR CHRISTIAN BEHAVIOR TOWARD OURSELVES (13:4–6)

The writer delivered these exhortations regarding believers' behavior toward ourselves.

"Marriage should be honored by all, and the marriage bed kept pure" (v. 4)

This is the clearest statement related to marriage and sexual ethics in the book of Hebrews. "God will judge the adulterer" (v. 4), but Christians are assured of escaping that judgment because God has called us not to sexual immorality but to purity. "The marriage bed," or sexual union, is extremely important to individuals, families, churches, nations, and society at large. Only as its sacredness is preserved can the institution of marriage be "honored" and kept pure.

"Nothing is to break the bond of marriage. God is deeply concerned about it, because a broken home will give an occasion for the enemies of God to delight in the tragic life of a Christian." (James T. Draper, *Hebrews*, 366.)

"Keep your lives free from the love of money" (v. 5)

Greed is a sickness of the soul, a malignancy in the spirit, a bottomless pit that Christians are to steer away from at all costs. The love of money is the root of all kinds of evil because it is a kind of addictive idolatry (1 Tim. 6:10). The more the greedy person gets, the more he or she wants.

Such a person is like the rich farmer in Jesus' parable who so lusted for increased possessions that he determined to tear down adequate barns in order to build even bigger ones.

Christians need not be anxious about money because the Lord is their helper.

To encourage his readers along these lines, the author quoted an Old Testament promise (Deut. 31:6 and in Josh. 1:5). The reason Christians should be content with what they have is that God has promised, "Never will I leave you; never will I forsake you."

■ *Christians are to (1) keep the marriage*
■ *union pure and to avoid sexual immorality;*
■ *and (2) keep their lives free from the love of*
■ *money. God offers the promise that He will*
■ *never leave Christians, and that promise*
■ *helps them to banish greed (v. 6).*

EXHORTATIONS FOR CHRISTIAN BEHAVIOR TOWARD GOD (13:7–9)

The writer delivered these exhortations regarding the believer's behavior toward God.

"Remember your leaders" (v. 7)

This is an admonition to honor and imitate those "who spoke the word of God" by which faith came. They are gone, but by their precept and example, they have left us firmly anchored to "Jesus Christ" who "is the same yesterday and today and forever" (v. 8).

"Do not be carried away by all kinds of strange teachings . . . be strengthened by grace" (v. 9)

This exhortation has to do with "foods" (v. 9). It is a warning against any new religious fad that foolishly focuses on foods while turning away from faith in God whose grace is uniquely mediated through Christ. Bread can sustain the body, but only grace can sustain the heart.

- *In these verses, the writer exhorted his read-*
- *ers to "remember your leaders" and "do not*
- *be carried away by all kinds of strange*
- *teachings." Instead, they are to be strength-*
- *ened by grace, not by regulations about food.*

SACRIFICES PLEASING TO GOD (13:10–16)

A spiritual sacrifice is an act done or given in the name of Christ for His glory. In the verses that follow, the writer mentioned several such sacrifices that are pleasing to God.

Christ's Supreme Sacrifice on the Cross (vv. 10–12)

Christ's sacrifice which He made outside the city gate (v. 12) does not require or involve or even allow any special meal. It is faith in Him alone on which the Christian's right relationship to God depends.

Our Sacrifice of Bearing Disgrace for Christ's Sake (vv. 13–14)

Here the writer called on Christians not to be at home where Jesus was homeless, not to get all settled down when Jesus had no place to lay His head, not to seek the world's praise when it has heaped abuse on our Lord, and not to cling so

Christ's Sacrifice

The book of Hebrews portrays Christ as the sinless High Priest who offered up Himself as a sacrifice for sinners (Heb 7:27). The superiority of Christ's sacrifice over the Levitical sacrificial system is seen in that His sacrifice had to be offered only once. First Peter 2 calls believers a holy and royal priesthood who offer up spiritual sacrifices. Jesus' death was an offering and sacrifice to God and, as such, a fragrant aroma (Eph. 5:2). Jesus was associated with the Passover sacrifice (1 Cor. 5:7).

selfishly to life inside the camp that we will not risk life outside the camp for Him who loved us and gave Himself for us.

Christians are to live always with the realization that "here we do not have an enduring city" (v. 14). Rather, they are a people who seek "the city which is to come."

Our Sacrifice of Praise to God (v. 15)

"Through Jesus, therefore, let us continually offer to God a sacrifice of praise—the fruit of lips that confess his name" (v. 15). Such an acceptable sacrifice of praise to God might also include, however, mouths that preach His gospel and lives that demonstrate His love. The "fruit of lips that confess his name" has always been the fruit of more believers, inasmuch as God's Word never returns to Him void.

Our Sacrifice of Self for the Sake of Others (v. 16)

"Do not neglect to do good and to share what you have" (v. 16, NRSV) is a powerful reminder that those who rail out against do-gooders are not on God's side. The alternatives to doing good are to do evil or to do nothing. Christians of every age do well to heed this call "to do good" and "to share" what we have. Such self-sacrifice is the authentication of the genuineness of the words of profession and confession which we have uttered with our mouths.

■ *The writer mentioned several sacrifices that*
■ *are pleasing to God. These include Christ's*
■ *supreme sacrifice on the Cross, the believer's*
■ *sacrifices of bearing abuse for Christ's sake,*
■ *sacrifice of praise to God, and sacrifice of self*
■ *for the sake of others.*

A COMMAND TO OBEY TO LEADERS (13:17)

The readers of Hebrews now receive advice on submitting to their leaders: "Obey your leaders and submit to their authority" (v. 17). This advice provides unqualified endorsement of Christian leaders in the particular fellowship to whom this letter was originally sent. The advice also intends to provide encouragement for the members to obey the teachings and to submit to the spiritual leadership of those who were called to keep watch over their souls "as men who must give an account" to God.

The special responsibility of church leaders is to be carried out joyfully: "Obey them so that their work will be a joy, not a burden" (v. 17). When a spirit of joy prevails, those in their spiritual charge are helped, comforted, reproved, and strengthened.

■ *Christians must follow the faith of their leaders by obeying them and submitting to their authority. When Christians submit to those who care for their spiritual needs, their leaders are free to do their jobs with joy, not with hardship or frustration.*

BENEDICTION AND CONCLUSION (13:18–25)

Benediction (vv. 18–20)

The writer of Hebrews exhorted his readers to "pray for us" (v. 18). He could make this request because he had a clear conscience in knowing that he desired to live honorably in every way toward his readers. Using the first person for the

There is a timelessness about this advice. God-called leaders are universally concerned for the highest interests of all the Christians to whom they are related. As a group, and individually, they provide spiritual direction for the community of faith. They rightly divide the word of truth and preach God's Word in season and out of season. They press the claims of Christ on both unbelievers who need to come to Him and on believers who need to come closer to Him. As the shepherd sleeplessly keeps watch over his flocks by night or as the soldier remains wakefully vigilant through the long watches of the night, so the spiritual leader is spiritually alert to discharge his pastoral responsibilities.

first time in his letter, he wrote, "I particularly urge you to pray so that I may be restored to you soon" (v. 19); that is, that he might quickly be with them again.

Conclusion (vv. 20–25)

The writer made a final appeal at the end of his letter. He asked his readers to "bear with my word of exhortation, for I have written you only a short letter" (v. 22). He shared the good news that Timothy had been released.

The readers were to greet all their leaders on behalf of the writer. He added that those from Italy send their greetings. Then with this beautifully simple word the letter is concluded, "Grace be with you all" (v. 25).

Because the most majestic and memorable benediction in the whole Bible is recorded in Hebrews 13:20–21, it is fitting to use it as the benediction for this look at the Book of Hebrews:

> "May the God of peace, who through the blood of the eternal covenant brought back from the dead our Lord Jesus, that great Shepherd of the sheep, equip you with everything good for doing his will, and may he work in us what is pleasing to him, through Jesus Christ, to whom be glory for ever and ever. Amen."

■ *The writer made a final appeal at the end of*
■ *his letter. He included, as part of his conclu-*
■ *sion, one of the most majestic and memorable*
■ *benedictions in the whole Bible (vv. 20–21).*

QUESTIONS TO GUIDE YOUR STUDY

1. The writer provided several final exhortations for his readers. What are his exhortations for Christian behavior toward others? Why is each so important?

2. What are the writer's exhortations for Christian behavior toward ourselves? Why is each so important?

3. What are the writer's exhortations for Christian behavior toward God? Why is each so important?

4. What spiritual sacrifices are pleasing to God?

5. Why does the writer issue a command for Christians to obey their spiritual leaders?

The following list is a collection of the sources used for this volume. All are from Broadman & Holman's list of published reference resources, to accommodate the reader's need for more specific information and or for an expanded treatment of Hebrews. All of these works will greatly aid in the reader's study, teaching, and presentation of the book of Hebrews. The accompanying annotations can be helpful in guiding the reader to the proper resources.

Adams, J. McKee, Rev. and Joseph A. Callaway, *Biblical Backgrounds*. This work provides valuable information on the physical and geographical settings of the New Testament. Its many colorful maps and other features add depth and understanding.

Blair, Joe, *Introducing the New Testament*, pp. 185–9. Designed as a core text for New Testament survey courses, this volume helps the reader in understanding the content and principles of the New Testament. Its features include special maps and photos, outlines, and discussion questions.

Cate, Robert L., *A History of the New Testament and Its Times*. An excellent and thorough survey of the birth and growth of the Christian faith in the first-century world.

Holman Bible Dictionary. An exhaustive, alphabetically arranged resource of Bible-related subjects. An excellent tool of definitions and other information on the people, places, things, and events.

Holman Bible Handbook, pp. 749–56. A comprehensive treatment that offers outlines, commentary on key themes and sections, and full-color photos, illustrations, charts, and maps. Provides an accent on the broader theological teachings.

Holman Book of Biblical Charts, Maps, and Reconstructions. A colorful, visual collection of charts, maps, and reconstructions, these well-designed tools are invaluable to the study of the Bible.

Lea, Thomas D., *The New Testament: Its Background and Message*, pp. 501–17. An excellent resource for background material—political, cultural, historical, and religious. Provides background information in both broad strokes on specific books, including the Gospels.

McQuay, Earl P., *Keys to Interpreting the Bible*. This work provides a fine introduction to the study of the Bible that is invaluable for home Bible studies, lay members of a local church, or students.

McQuay, Earl P., *Learning to Study the Bible*. This study guide presents a helpful procedure that employs the principles basic to effective and thorough Bible study. Using Philippians as a model, the various methods of Bible study are applied. Excellent for home Bible studies, lay members of a local church, and students.

Robertson, A. T., *A Grammar of the Greek New Testament in the Light of Historical Research*. An exhaustive, scholarly work on the underlying language of the New Testament. Provides advanced insights into the grammatical, syntactical, and lexical aspects of the New Testament.

Robertson, A. T., *Word Pictures in the New Testament*, "The Epistle of Hebrews," vol. 5, 325–451. This six-volume series provides insights into the language of the New Testament Greek. Provides word studies as well as grammatical and background insights into the epistles of Paul.

Valentine, Foy, *Hebrews, James, 1, 2 Peter* (Layman's Bible Book Commentary, vol. 23), pp. 13–65. A popular-level treatment of the book of Hebrews. This easy-to-use volume provides a relevant and practical perspective for the reader.

SHEPHERD'S NOTES

_____

_____

_____

_____

_____

_____

_____

_____

_____

_____

_____

_____

_____

_____

_____

_____

_____

_____

SHEPHERD'S NOTES

SHEPHERD'S
NOTES

_____

_____

_____

_____

_____

_____

_____

_____

_____

_____

_____

_____

_____

_____

_____

_____

_____